All the world's a stage,

And all the men and women merely players;

They have their exits and their entrances;

And one man in his time plays many parts,

His acts being seven ages.

Shakespeare, As You Like It,
(1599, Act 2 -Scene 7).

Published by Gregory Institute of
Transactional Analysis

Mandurah, Western Australia,
Australia 6208

E mail.   lgregory@iinet.net.au

www.drlindagregory.com.au

Phone   61 8 9537 8768   Fax 61 8 9537 6518
Mobile 0409 687 926

A catalogue of this book is with the WA State Library.
ISBN 978-0-646-49796-9

Cover design by Linda Gregory
Art Production by Goran Gasic

Abstract

This workbook explores our inherited and developed belief systems, and how they have shaped and manifested what is in our lives at present. I will refer to these as scripts, a term I've embraced over a generation of study and practice of Transactional Analysis.

Most people want to create abundance and happiness in their lives, but don't realize that early negative beliefs about self, others and the quality of life, their scripts, may well be blocking positive intentions. Unconscious beliefs carry strong energy vibrations that may well sabotage what we are choosing to manifest on a conscious level.

The law of attraction is currently being talked about in wide circles; and science, particularly quantum physics, is proposing that our consciousness plays a part in creating our world.

This book will explore how to identify old beliefs from the past that may have been blocking efforts to manifest in the present, then will offer some experiential exercises into how to clear the past and use the law of attraction. Our present state of consciousness creates our world, either positively, or negatively. This book will help you direct intentions to positive outcomes.

You will find understanding about your past issues and past experiences and how to change them. Using techniques from Transactional Analysis, such as Redecision therapy, Self Reparenting, and learning to connect with and care for your inner Child, you can clear your past and move forward into the present and future, and manifest happiness in your life.

I will offer a literature review of several writers on these subjects that I have found useful and interesting. Many writers as well as myself, say our past needs to be cleared in order for us to fully connect with and live from our spiritual selves. Living in the Now rather than stuck in the past or worrying about the future is our path to happiness. Happiness is what we all seek and deserve. A burning question is, What brings us happiness?

In the final chapter you will learn a series of steps you can use to manifest your positive intentions.

CONTENTS

Part 2
Neuroscience

Part 3
Manifestation

My thanks to my editors, Gary and Judy.

My forever gratitude to the many teachers,
authors, husband, family and friends,
and to the Universe, who have all been a
guiding part of my journey in life.

Past, Present

& Future

Workbook for,

Clearing the past, for living in the present

and manifesting your future.

Linda Gregory, Ph.D.

Forward

I have been drawn to write this book, instructed to in fact, by my intuition, or universe guides, whatever the case may be. It has been in my head for many years. I came to psychotherapy training twenty-five years ago, and at that time I had been meditating for fifteen years. My focus at that time was to bring meditation, spirituality, and therapy together in some way. However, when I spoke about that to my teacher, he said it was magical thinking and totally discounted my ideas. From his reaction I decided to put it away for a while, until the time was right to come back to it. Now the time is right. I have learned and experienced much more. Science is now talking more about Quantum physics, and how our minds work. The Law of Attraction is being talked about in wide circles. It seems our collective spiritual awareness is on a rapid increase.

My challenge with this book is going to be where to begin and where to end. There is so much interesting information and scientific discovery happening that I would like to write about all of it (in my usual drive to be perfect and work hard). However, if I attempt to do that I will never finish. I have been in the position of saying to myself, 'I don't know enough yet. I'm not an expert on all the facts with science. It will take me years to research it all and write about it with enough knowledge.' All that is to some extent true. However, I do know psychotherapy after twenty-five years of experience in working with people. I do know how spirituality has been a part of my life, and the importance of that for many people.

In the field of psychotherapy I believe an important part of my job is to assist people who are wanting more of a personal spiritual connection to find their own way of interacting with spirit, energy, the universe, God, what ever you are comfortable in naming it. I do know about Transactional Analysis (TA) and how that theory can be used very effectively to help people understand why they feel like they do, understand their behaviour, and how to make changes. I am a Transactional Analysis (TA) psychotherapist, and a TA trainer and supervisor, and have been for twenty-five years. So I will mainly be drawing on that knowledge in this book. I will also add other theories that I have learned along the way.

For over thirty years I have been reading books on topics I will explore in this book. There are a wide variety of books. It can be very confusing, and at times I have felt as if I was going in too many directions. What are they all saying? Some say one way is the way to go, or the right answer, others advise a different direction. They all seem to say 'this is the way.' I have now come to the conclusion that most are saying the same thing. Perhaps in different language, but basically aiming in the same direction. The idea about the importance of positive thinking is not new. Many writers, some of whom I will discuss, have been talking about our need to think positively.

My wish for this book is to put it all together in a simple and readable style. I will share with you what I have found for myself to work best. I hope for some readers this will save you time by not having to read 'all' the books out there. By all means read widely, but first get your main process of change happening, create positive thinking as much as possible, create happiness in your life by finding out what real happiness is, and manifest your wants and goals. Then you can go back and read the theory in detail if you wish.

The foolish man seeks happiness in the distance, the wise man grows it under his feet. James Oppenheim

There are three sections to this book.
Part one is clearing the past.
Part two is the position science plays.
Part three is guidance in finding your own personal path to happiness, and using the Law of Attraction to manifest your dreams and reach your full potential.

Past, Present, & Future

Clearing the past, for living in the present and manifesting your future.

❦❦❦❦❦❦

Chapter One
Introduction

Think positively and you can create all you ever want and dream about. Change the way you look at things and the things you see will change. People like the Dalai Lama, W. Dyer, J. Demartini, D. Chopra, *What the Bleep Do We Know* movie, T*he Secret,* C. Tipping, E. Tolle, J. Krishnamurti, Maharishi, Mehesh, Yogi, L. MacTaggert, and many others all say this. From Jesus onwards, perhaps even before him, this message has been put forward. It is not new. You only need to change your thinking and be positive and you can create your dreams and goals. It sounds so easy. However, for many people there are blocks and habitual negative patterns to clear first. Old belief systems that have been ingrained for years don't just disappear overnight. Recent neuroscience studies by L. Cozolino, Professor of Psychology at Pepperdine University, (*The Neuroscience of Psychotherapy,* 2002) tell us those repetitive patterns of thinking result in habitual synapse connections. Therefore, it takes some time and practice to break the old patterns and create new positive ones. So when some people look at all the new books, movies, advice directions and attempt to put it into practice, it often does not work immediately. Often the person gets discouraged then stops. They give up and go back to old beliefs of, 'see, this stuff does not work for me. I'm not able to do this. I'm useless. This is all a bunch of nonsense!' This is discouraging to say the least. What you need to understand is that it does work; however, for many it takes time to clear unconscious negative beliefs and blocks that have been part or your life for many years.

Indeed, many of our old beliefs and patterns have been defence mechanisms and have helped us survive. If our inner Child ego state relinquished these survival tactics too quickly we would quite possibly feel very scared. Be easy on yourself. Give yourself time to make these changes, and learn how to take care of your inner Child while making the required changes and practising the new ways. Also keep in mind while reading this book that positive thinking does not mean we will never feel sad, angry, unhappy or any of the other so-named negative feelings. They are a part of who we are, and a part of life. We need to learn how to let those feelings have their life and manage them. We need to learn to simply be present with them.

For myself, I have had many issues and stuck spots to clear along my journey, and indeed, still have issues that come up. When teaching and working with clients, I often get an enlightening Mument of self awareness, and realize that I have some other issue to deal with and change. I find that exciting and interesting. I think life would become dull, colourless, and boring, if any other way. I don't think we ever reach a point that we can say, there - I am done. I certainly hope not. I find change and growth challenging, fun, and exciting.

It is my hope and intent that this book will be an assistance to you to uncover old patterns and beliefs, and be of help for you to find ways to change what you choose to change, and for you to find the life that you want to lead. We are all looking for happiness, and the Dalai Lama says that is the purpose of life. A question we need to ask ourselves is, 'What brings happiness?' Is it gaining more and more material things? Or is it living a meaningful life in which we reach our full potential and use our core strengths and skills? Is it when we are connected to our soul, our spiritual self?

The Celestine Prophecy says that the past must be cleared in order to move further along with spiritual development. This is one of my main focuses when doing therapy with people. I have learned to be patient while clients begin to feel safe to make changes. For me this has been a challenge and a growth. One of my drivers being to hurry and get things done, (more about where that came from for me will come later), I have had to slow down and go at the pace of clients. I have learned to honour the defence constructs of the Child and understand the need to hang on to them for as long as needed for the Child to feel safe, to trust, and to make changes.

Therein lies another frustration. Time. It does take time for these changes to be integrated, and recent directions for counselling and psychotherapy are short-term, quick-fix, limited sessions, limited costs, and brief therapy. Governments and insurance companies are limiting the number of sessions to usually six - twelve sessions per client. Where are we going? Deep psychotherapy and spiritual growth usually always takes longer than twelve sessions.

Neuroscience is showing that the brain does have plasticity, and new synapse connections can be made, but it does take a number of times to repeatedly do things in different ways for new connections to develop. Then old ones can fall away or become un-wired. People need to be supported through this process.

In the last century, Carl Jung, famous psychoanalyst who studied with Freud, talked about the main goal of therapy being to start or advance a client on their spiritual connection or journey. Now it seems for many therapists that goal has been lost or shackled by regulations to do short term work. The focus is now short- term, quick-fix of the day-to-day problems, and then finish with therapy. In many cases, in my view, there is not even time to deal with the presenting issues, let alone any deeper work for the inner Child, inner spirit and soul connection work. Our fast-paced life and quick-fix attitude has resulted in many people losing their sense of self, and connection to their higher power, the universe, or spirit, as well as loss of connection with others and partners.

The result seems to be that an increasing number of people are feeling depressed and anxious. I find it alarming that so many young people as well as adults are on anti-depressants. In my view, a large part of this growing societal depression and anxiety is due to loss of spiritual connection and the chase for material possessions that are thought to bring happiness. Carl Jung allegedly purported years ago that loss of personal connection to spirit created problems. Many people he said, sensing their loss, turned to alcohol in an attempt to fill the gap; that's why the name 'spirits' was given to alcohol.

People find. when they do obtain material gains, that their 'happiness' is short lived. It does not last. Then sadness or dissatisfaction returns. We, for the most part in our society, have not found what real happiness is or how to obtain it.

Spiritual connection takes many forms. There is inner connection to our sense of self, who we are, our I-am-ness, knowing that spirit resides within us. Extending from that is what our direction to reach our full potential is, and connection to our higher spiritual self, or the Universe, whatever you are comfortable naming it. There is connection to others, knowing we are all one, intimacy with family and friends, neighbours, community, and having a sense of being important, and a sense of belonging. When we inwardly obtain that sense of connection it will thenspread outward to all others, to other countries. We need to be aware that we are all one, made of the same energy. Instead of warring between nations and peoples we could experience love for each other and promote non-violence and peace.

Definition

I have learned from many years of tertiary study that when writing about a topic, one needs to begin with a definition. There are so many concepts and names, what do I mean by spirituality? When I talk of spirituality what I mean is not attached to a specific religion. In my opinion, many religions have lost the essence of spirit. For me the words God, spirit, universe, energy, love, source intelligence, all mean the same. At this point in my life, 'God' to my way of thinking is perhaps the scientific intelligent energy, rather than the idea of a supreme being in human form. Is it possible that 'God' is the master intelligence that created, maintains with love, and is behind, The Theory of Everything that scientists are looking for. We are all a part of this same energy. All that exists is this energy. This energy has always been there, will always be there, is everywhere, and is within all things. Science tells us that all matter, is made up of hydrogen, nitrogen, oxygen and carbon. Tolle, noted spiritual writer, and many other writers, describe this by saying we are one consciousness (2005, p.4).

I have experienced many clients coming to therapy saying they feel lost, don't know who they are, and want to find themselves. I think at least part of what they are experiencing is a disconnection from their spirit or their energy.

Since I too am limited in the number of clients I can work with personally, and the number of sessions I can provide, I have decided to find another way to help. My aim with this book is to assist people who want to re-connect to their spirit. This book is for people to read as a self-help book to clear old blocks and beliefs in order to find their spirit, learn how to reach their full potential, and to manifest all that they choose to in their lives.

When the blocks are cleared, it is then about people experiencing how to use their minds and thinking in a more positive way to stop creating the same negative patterns in their lives over and over again. Thinking creates reality. Change the way you see things, and the things you see will change (Dyer, 1997).

It's all about belief! What you believe about self, others and the quality of life is how it will always be for you: until you change those beliefs. Life always reflects our beliefs.

The universe brings us what we ask for, consciously and unconsciously, and it brings lessons we need to learn. From my own experience, the first time the universe wants us to learn something, it gives us an easy bump on the head to offer us the opportunity to change; if we don't take that chance bumps get harder and harder until we do learn and make changes.

For example, when people are doing too much and over-working the first bump is tiredness. If they don't slow down, the second bump is becoming 'vertically' ill. What I mean by that is they may get colds, flu or overtired but they are still upright on their feet, vertical, and therefore can soldier on. If they still don't slow down, going further towards burnout, they start to feel stressed, sad, cry for no apparent reason, and some form of depression manifests itself. If they still don't take notice of the bumps and slow down, they will get horizontally ill. That is, not on their feet, but horizontal on their backs in bed. Recovery from the horizontal position takes longer. Much better to make changes with the first bump, and be grateful for the bump.

Some people don't make changes or learn lessons in this lifetime, and that is OK. Our free will that was given to us is always honoured. For example, if a person believes they are not lovable, they will keep attracting partners who don't love them, or attract abusive people. If a person believes life is a hard struggle, that is how it will be for them.

Alternatively we can, as E. Tolle instructs, become enlightened, re-gain our innate awareness, be autonomous, and be fully present in life. Once we gain presence in our life, listening to the 'still small voice inside', we can sense the divine essence of life.

Tolle asks the question, which I have paraphrased, Can we rise above identification with our ego that condemns us to imprisonment within our past beliefs? The answer to that question is what this book is about.

Chapter Two
Introduction to
Transactional Analysis

I will begin to discuss change from a Transactional Analysis point of view. How do people become who they are? Why do they do what they do? Is it nature or nurture? Is it the genes, personality, and temperament you were born with, or is it the result of your childhood experiences and how you were parented or cared for by others. A. Shore, Ph.D., University of California, (2003), in his writings says it is 100% of both. Certainly genes, DNA, and temperament are a part of it. Neuroscience now tells us that people are born with certain possibilities for both positive development and negative conditions to eventuate. However, the question whether they eventuate or not depends on whether experiences happen that trigger their onset, or development. We are not hard-wired from birth. Our brains have plasticity and can change and develop according to our experiences.

I don't want to get lost in science too much because there is so much interesting information coming out each year that I could write forever. I will leave you to read in more depth, and I will offer some suggestions along the way. However, I will be saying more on this topic later. There are many aspects to TA theory and each offers another insight into one's self and how you became who you are today. Let us start from the beginning. I believe sometime after conception, and before birth, messages were felt from your mother about what she was feeling, whether you were wanted or not, whether your mother was relaxed or tense, happy or unhappy, and was your father present or not, and what was his feeling about you arriving. This is of course pre-verbal. A baby does not think in words, it is all at a feeling level. R. Goulding, a psychiatrist and co-founder of Redecision therapy, and one of my wonderful TA trainers many years ago, said there are negative feelings that a baby can be born with. These feelings can later become negative beliefs about self that can take three forms:

1. I was not wanted and should not have been born.
2. I was born the wrong sex.
3. I was born at the wrong time.

Often parents or other family members may have said things to the child, not meaning to be hurtful, but not realizing the negative impact those messages made on the child. Things such as, 'you were a change-of-life baby and not meant to have happened; you came along too late; you were supposed to be a boy; your father wanted a boy; Your mother wanted a girl; you were a mistake; you came too early.' The responsibility for conception, birth, and gender was positioned on the child. And, of course we all know who was responsible for the conception: the parents who had sex; not the child. Additionally, it is the male sperm that determines the sex of the child. How many wives over centuries have been blamed, and some killed, for not producing a male? Sadly, many people have started their lives with one or all of those beliefs about self.

From here we will look further at early scripting and how that process works. As I talk about scripting I often refer to 'parents'. It is important to keep in mind that scripting happens not only from parents as in mother and father, but also parent figures such as foster parents, grandparents, older siblings, teachers, peers, and experiences at school, such as being teased or bullied. Society, state, and religion also can play an important role in scripting.

Transactional Analysis theory says scripting involves the ego states of people. We all have three ego states or parts to our personality, being the Parent, Adult and Child. These ego states developed as we grew according to both the DNA we were born with and the environment in which we were raised. The nature/ nurture argument that has been going on for ever argues about which is responsible for how a person develops. Was it the DNA or personality traits we were born with, and therefore fixed and unchangeable, or was it the result of how we were raised? The reality is that both are involved.

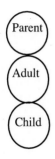

Parent Ego State composed of messages which are taught & recorded from parents and other parent figures. Behaviour is either critical or nurturing.

Adult gathers information, makes decisions, functions like a computer. Here & now thinking.

Composed of messages which were felt from inside self. Wants and needs. Real self.

Functional Ego States
Parent is either Nurturing, warm & caring (NP), or Critical, aggressive & controlling, (CP).

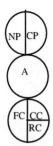

Child is either conforming, complying, (CC) and doing as told, or Rebellious (RC) and not doing as told. Free Child (FC) is being real self and doing as one wishes based on self wants and needs. Spontaneous and fun loving. Expresses real feelings.   (Berne, 1992).

Ego States

The Parent (Berne, 1964, 1972) ego state consists of behaviours, thoughts and feelings copied from our parents and parent figures, and the 'shoulds' we learned from them. This is where many of our belief systems are filed, many of which came from our parent figures. They told us how to be, not be, and what to believe. Our Parent ego state consists largely of who these parent figures were historically.

The Adult ego state has behaviours, thoughts and feelings from here-and-now that we deal with each day. This is where we think from, plan, and run our lives.

The Child ego state has behaviour, thoughts and feelings replayed from childhood, (E. Berne, 1964, 1972), historically who we were in the past. Experiences and memories from our childhood are stored in our Child ego state. I believe our Child state also contains our real self, and is the home of our spiritual beings, where we first connect with the universal energy. The Child contains our intuition and it is through the Child that we achieve our potential and mission for life. James Hillman in his book *The Soul's Code* (noted in *The Celestine Vision*, p.106) says 'we all came in with character and calling. But the fog of birth obscures this self-understanding, and the struggles of childhood can often be intense and fearful. As children we lose our sure connection with divine love and energy.'

E. Berne, M. James, L. Gregory, P. Clarkson, and others have talked about Physis energy. Physis is our core energy, the force of nature, and by definition means the ability to eternally grow or become more perfect. I believe we are born with this energy and according to one's beliefs we could say that this is the energy that we bring from past lives. At birth perhaps, a baby still has knowledge and connection to the spirit world but soon loses it for many reasons. Physis energy originates from within the Child ego state and from there permeates into all ego states, then outwards to the world around us. We are all connected to each other within this energy field, and of course we effect each other and the world through this energy.

Growth and change are spontaneous and begin from within. The Stoics, members of an ancient philosophical school, saw all that exists as being affected by change. Change must always occur; that is life itself. Physis could be said to be our God force within. Physis energy then is a powerful internal force striving towards growth and to become all that we are meant to be. It is an upward force that begins in the Child ego state and in spite of the downward force of the negative script messages, physis strives to continue towards growth. We have all seen in life how some people overcome the most difficult experiences and histories to reach greatness and success. This transformational potential is inherent in all of us.

This book is about helping you to come back to your sense of connection to this energy, recovering your initial character and calling, to get past the scripting that created the fog and to reconnect to your pure core spiritual self. E. Berne, founder of Transactional Analysis, in the 60s talked about our innate rights to autonomy, which is our birthright. Contained in autonomy is our capacity for awareness, spontaneity, and intimacy. Freeing ourselves from our past also means re-connecting to these fundamental capacities. Being aware of what is, in the Mument, rather than locked in the past: aware of the Now, rather than identified with our endless thoughts, brings us to be open to the divine inside us. We allow the divine to manifest through us. Being free to act spontaneously can bring joy and happiness. The capacity to be intimate with others is what love is about. This is our goal and purpose.

> *The place to be happy is here, the time to be*
> *happy is now.*
> *Robert Ingersoll*

As I mentioned, scripting begins from conception. Scripting is the life plan that you decided on from an early age. This plan is put together from the messages and directions you were given, or that you perceived you were given, as you grew. When

I say 'perceived you were given', what I mean is that sometimes parents say something that children misinterpret. For example, a large part of my own scripting came from my mother, who was often stressed on working days. If I did not have my chores done when she got home, she was angry. Understandably so. To avoid her anger I decided I would have to 'hurry up' and get the work done. This then became a 'Hurry Up' driver for me throughout life. To this day, I still have difficulty accepting not getting things done. It has at times been a positive in my life as it has led to success and achievement.

By the time you were four to seven years old the main components of your script were in place. After seven you continued to polish the elements. Like all stories it had a beginning, middle and an end, and had main casts and characters. As Shakespeare said, 'All the world's a stage...'

Throughout this process you made many decisions about how you should be or not be, what you should do or not do, and how your life would turn out, what the final scene would likely be. By seven you had decided on three very important aspects to your life. A decision about your self, for example 'I am good' or 'I am bad.' A decision about others, such as who are 'good people, or scary, or better than you, or not to be trusted.' Decisions were made about life, such as, 'life is wonderful' or 'life is a struggle'. All these decisions can take many forms and combinations.

Once these decisions are made people tend to be very stubborn, and like to prove their decisions right rather than wrong. They like to have examples which validate their beliefs in order to say, 'see...that always happens to me!' Be it positive or negative, we like familiarity. E. Berne talked about our innate human structure hunger. Humans hunger for their lives to be structured, organized, and predictable. We are usually not comfortable with the unknown. We like to know what is going to happen and when. Change is often difficult so we strive to keep things the same, that which is known and therefore comfortable.

The new can be scary because we have not yet experienced it. The old, even though negative, can be like a comfortable old coat. We know what it feels like, and it feels like it belongs to us. This is me! The script culminates in a payoff; an early decision as to how your life will end. Will you end up alone and unloved or part of a loving family and friends, successful or not?

The important aspect to script is that it is decisional. You have made all the decisions; they have not been made for you. Even though it was parents or parent figures that told you how you should be or what you should do, it was you who decided to comply or not. That means that you can change those decisions. You don't have to wait for someone else to change, or someone to give you permission to change. You have the power to do that for yourself.

It's true that you may have made those decisions at an early age for good reasons, in order to survive and get along with the people you lived with. You may have had to find a way to survive as best you could. A three-or-four-year-old does not have the power to walk up to parents and say, 'I don't like what is going on here, so I am moving out'. You had to find a way to protect yourself, to stay safe, to be loved, and consequently had to please them. As I said, the decisions about script were yours; nevertheless, there may have been a great deal of pressure on you to decide in a certain way. There may have been consequences if you did not do as they said. Living with the risk of abuse, not being loved, being ignored, losing privileges, all put pressure on children to conform and adapt in certain ways.

Likewise, decisions made as a child to survive or simply please parents may have been good decisions at that time; however, as an adult they may not be so useful. Those early decisions may well cause problems, get in the way, and cause blocks to your spiritual growth and achievement of the success you deserve. Old unconscious beliefs, for example, that life is a struggle, may well result is life continuing to be a struggle. One hard thing after another seems to keep happening. That is not the way life should be: life is meant to be joyful, happy, abundant and successful. That is the birthright for all of us.

What are the many components that make up our scripts?

The main components are drivers and injunctions. Each form a set of decisions that children make in order to get along with people around them. Another important aspect to those decisions are that they are made in response to their perceptions of what is going in their world. A child does not have the capacity to see all the facts and usually does not have an understanding of all the reasons for what parents are doing or not doing, saying or not saying. Often, later in life, a person can look back on what has happened and say, 'I now understand why Mum did that, or why Dad was feeling like he did'.

Decisions are often made based on limited knowledge and understanding of what is happening. Keep in mind that for some parents, they did make mistakes whilst believing they were doing parenting the best way. Most parents did the best they could with what they knew at the time. A relatively few number of parents or parent figures were deliberately abusive and hurtful. Some parents may be in denial about what they did or did not do, and for people who had those parents it is important for the person to believe in themselves, and know what they know. I urge people to find a good therapist to achieve the healing they need so that they can get on with living life now. Don't stay a victim.

Drivers are messages that parents give a child about how they should perform in life in order to survive and do well. These messages can be given verbally or non-verbally, or a combination of both. Modeling is a powerful way of giving a message. For example my Dad often verbally told me it was good to work hard, and he modelled that by doing the same himself. He usually worked six days a week for twelve to fourteen hours a day.

Young children have acute perceptions of how their parents are feeling. You have all probably watched your children or others as they discovered their world. When children are introduced to new experiences they will look at Mum or Dad to see the expression on their face. 'Do they think this is OK?' they are wondering, If Mum has a worried or scared look the child may decide, no I'm not doing this, Mum thinks it is scary.

The Drivers are messages that come from Mum and Dad's Parent ego state and form the Parent ego state of the child. When parents say things such as, 'Be strong, hurry up, we will be late, be top of the class, get your work done, if you loved me you would do as I want,' the child puts those rules into their Parent ego state and they become the Drivers. The most common Drivers that are part of Transactional Analysis theory are: Be Perfect, Be Strong, Try Hard, Please me and others, Hurry up.

The child then feels a compulsion to obey these rules. These rules are not completely harmful: at times it is good to work hard, or please others; however when a person feels that have to do this all the time at the expense of themselves, and feel fear if they are not obeying the rules, then it is too much.

I will present some examples of how drivers effect people's lives. Throughout the book I will write about my own experience, and present some case examples. None of the names are real. I will also do not put in any indentifying information about people in order to maintain confidentiality. We will be introduced to the people here and then re-visit them later in the book to illustrate the progress of their stories, and we will see how their script has impacted on their lives.

Ann, an attractive professional woman, grew up in a family where success was important. Both her parents were high achievers and worked hard. When Ann came home from school with a report that had five A's and one B the critical response from her father was, 'Why didn't you get an A in that subject?' So Ann, feeling hurt, decided that she had to work hard for perfection, and if she was not perfect at just about everything, she was not OK. Later in life she now works herself much too hard, is stressed, and has suffered from burnout. Her father could have said, 'Well done for getting five A's, that is great.'

Her twenty-year marriage has problems because she is away from home a great deal of the time, working late hours. Her children complain that she does not have enough fun time with them. Her Adult understands that she is working too much; however, her Child ego state still feels scared if she stops. She starts to feel worthless again when she slows down, as she did with her father.

Betty, a tense looking person, grew up with a father who was often angry, and scared his children as well as his wife. At times he would get violent and hit Betty's mother and the children. That was of course terrifying to all of them. Betty learned to become hypervigilant. She was always watchful of Dad, reading his moods, seeing if he was angry. She did her best to keep him happy by pleasing him as much as she possibly could in order to stay safe and keep her Mum and siblings safe. When Betty was little this was helpful as it did at times prevent Dad from being violent. It did not work all the time.

Now in Betty's life she still feels she has to please others, especially men. It is hard work to be hypervigilant all the time. Betty is tense and has irritable bowel syndrome, causing her great distress. She rarely gives any time to herself, and rarely feels relaxed.

Bob, as a little boy, came home from school one day crying because he was being teased at school. His father, rather than comforting Bob, got angry and told him firmly that if he ever let boys bully and tease him again or came home crying that he would belt him. Bob learned to be strong and hold his feelings in, and to fight with others at school. He in fact became a bully, thinking this would please his Dad, and in fact it did. His Dad was an aggressive man who bullied his team at work and had the attitude of being pleased when Bob was becoming like him. This caused Bob problems at school, and later in his marriage. His wife complained that he never showed any feelings, other than anger, and was always fighting and aggressive with her.

In my own scripting, if I did not do as Mum wanted she became angry and would not talk to me for days. I felt shunned, unloved and bad, so I decided to always please her and do what she wanted. From my Dad I took on the Work Hard driver, and from Mum, I took the Please Me, and Be Perfect drivers. For many years, I was driven to work hard and please others, until I made some changes.

With scripting, a person can decide to take on messages and conform, or they can go the opposite way and rebel. For example, a child can rebelliously decide, 'I'm not going to do what Dad tells me to do'. This decision can later get transferred to others in life. For instance, a man who made this decision might well transfer it onto other men in his life such as his boss, and not do what he is asked. Obviously this will cause him problems in his career. On the other hand, when a person conforms they do as they are told. When I decided to please Mum, I later felt I had to please my partner by working hard, when in fact he wanted me to slow down. If a person rebels against a parent message as a child, then he may transfer that to his partner and rebel against things she asks him to do. For example, 'Will you do....', he replies, 'Don't tell me what to do'.

Injunctions

Injunctions are the messages that come from the parent's Child ego state and become embedded in the child's Child ego state. The twelve injunctions are: Don't Be or Exist, Don't Be You, Don't Be a Child, Don't Grow Up, Don't Succeed, Don't (do anything), Don't Be Important, Don't Belong, Don't be Close, Don't Be Well, Don't Think, Don't Feel.

Again these messages can be verbal or non-verbal and are messages of how not to be. They are messages that come from parents' fears. They represent what parents may have been frightened of for themselves and for their child. They can be aspects of the child's personality that the parents may not be comfortable with. It is often aspects of the child that the parent was not allowed to have when they were little.

For example, Carol was often scolded when she was playing and having fun; her stern mother would tell her to go get her work done. 'Haven't you got something you need to be doing,' Mum would say. Carol decided that the only way she was going to be OK with Mum was when she was working. Carol meticulously cleaned the kitchen, cleaned the cupboards, cooked, and kept her room spotless to please her mother. Later in life when she had children she found that she felt that same old fear return when her children were playing and having fun. She heard herself saying to her children (even though she had decided to never emulate her mother) 'Haven't you got something you need to be doing?' thus passing the same script onto her children.

Bob and Mary Goulding, founders of Redecision therapy, found these twelve injunctions to be present in client's scripts. I have also found these 'don't' messages to be present in most of my client's scripts. At times there are even some different ones to the ones listed here.

Bob and Mary, who were and are wonderful psychotherapists, developed the model of Redecision therapy which clears scripts very effectively. This is a very powerful way of helping people change old unhealthy decisions into new decisions that will result in a better life for the person.

For example, Ann above, who at a young age decided she had to be perfect and work hard in order to be OK, could redecide that old decision into a new decision for herself that she is fine as she is, and does not have to work hard all the time or be perfect in order to be loved and OK.

We will have a look at what these injunctions may entail.

Bill grew up with a angry critical father who was violent and abusive. Bill was the youngest of five children, and he always felt that he was unwanted by his father. He often heard his father say things to his mother like, 'If you hadn't had all these kids things would be better around here'. His father took no responsibility for the birth of the children, blaming their presence on his wife. Bill was often criticized by his father for most everything he did. He felt he was never praised or complimented. His older siblings learned from their father to be critical, and they also criticized Bill as well as their mother.

Bill's belief was that he should not have been born, and

that his father would have been happier if he did not exist. Sadly, Bill decided that if things got bad enough he would kill himself. He went though much of his life feeling suicidal and not really understanding where that came from until he came to therapy.

Bill's redecision work was to imagine seeing his angry father in an empty chair in front of him in my office where he was safe, and to remember a time when he was small, and his father was being abusive. Next step was to tell his father, using his Child ego state, that he did not like his father's anger and that he had a right to exist. He also told his father that it was his responsibility that Bill was born, and that he was born a male. Bill as well told his father that he had a right to live and live happily and that he was not going to ever feel suicidal again. Bill felt relieved after that work and was then ready to make other changes once he had decided to stay alive.

Another example was Jill, the youngest of seven children in a Catholic family. Her mother had become tired and ill when she discovered that she was pregnant again. Her Child ego state was internally screaming, 'Not another one'. Jill experienced these thoughts her mother was having and felt her mother was never happy at having Jill around, and in fact at one point tried to kill Jill. Jill often felt suicidal, especially when she felt she was in the way or not wanted. When Jill understood where the feeling came from she then decided to live happily which is her birthright, as it is for all people.

Some people have given themselves the Don't Exist message because they believe they are worthless. If a child feels angry and ignored when a little brother or sister was born, then that child can decide she is bad and deserves to die. Or if a mother tells a son, 'You nearly killed me when you were born because you were so big', then he may take the responsibility for being born, and being a big baby, and decide he was bad and should die. Berne called this the Torn Mother script.

An example of the Don't be You message was unhappy Carol whose parents said to her many times, we want you to be a lawyer like your cousin. You are intelligent and that is what you are going to do. Carol was not remotely interested in becoming a lawyer. She was interested in animals and wanted a career in that field. Carol's parents were angry when she mentioned that, and thus Carol strongly felt they were saying 'don't be who or what you want to be, you have to be who we want you to be.' Carol did become a lawyer and hated it. It was never her choice or passion for what she wanted to do.

Lynn experienced another example of a Don't be You injunction. When she was born her parents had wanted a boy. She was often told by her mother that she was meant to be a boy because they already had a girl and her father wanted a boy. Lynn decided to be as much like a boy as she could and became a tom-boy. She did not like dolls, she wanted trucks and boy toys. She learned to use the tools in her Dad's workshop and often helped him with what he was doing. When Lynn was seven, her parents had a baby boy, and then Lynn felt useless and in the way. In her mind she thought, 'Mum and Dad have the older daughter, and now the son, so I am not needed or wanted.' The middle-child syndrome often affects children this way. In order to feel worthwhile in her family she felt she had to be better than her sister and brother. She learned to be helpful to her Mother, she became a good cook, she kept her room cleaner than her sister's, she was the 'good child'. Lynn often in her life felt she had to be better than others and achieve more in order to be valuable. She did achieve, but at the expense of working too hard and not having enough fun time for herself. She later decided to slow down, and decided that she was a valued and loved person for who she is.

Don't be a Child was shown in Lynn's script as well when she described how she experienced unease when she and her sister and brother were playing and having fun. Their Mother would often say angrily, 'Haven't you kids got some chores to get done, stop being so rambunctious'. The covert message from her Mum was stop being children, even though they were children.

The family history of Lynn's mother was that she was orphaned when she was ten years of age and probably had to grow up fast and care for herself. She most likely decided, with some reality, that if she remained a child she might not survive. Therefore when Lynn's mother later had her children she became scared when her children were being childlike and having fun. In an irrational kind of way Lynn's Mum was protecting them. Mum was unconsciously thinking, 'I have to stop my kids from being children so they learn to survive.'

Another example was Tom, who was the oldest of four in his family. His Mum and Dad often argued and he felt he might have been the cause for being naughty or in the way. He decided that he should try to fix things so they would not have anything to fight about. He worked hard at trying to make everything right in the house. He was also often told by his parents, 'You are the oldest and you have to set a good example for the younger ones.' Tom decided to hurry up and grow up, and stop being a child. In adulthood Tom is very serious, hardworking, and successful, but sad, tense and lacking fun and friendships in his life.

The opposite was true for Sam, who was the youngest in Tom's family. Since their mother and father did not have a close relationship, his mother became overly attached to Sam being the youngest. She used Sam to fill her needs for close connection and the messages she gave Sam were, Don't Grow up and leave me, stay here with me and keep me company. Sam, now in his forties, still lives with his mother and has never married. He is still very immature, childlike, and does not responsibly manage his life. His mother does many things for him. At some level Sam knows he is pleasing his mother by staying childlike.

Laura (also quite childlike in manner) was born to a mother who had lost a child through stillbirth before Laura. When she was born her mother was still very depressed and unstable. When Laura was three her mother attempted to kill herself and Laura by turning on the car in a locked garage with a hose inserted in the car. Thankfully someone heard Laura's loud screams and saved them. Her mother was taken into care and a kind aunt took Laura to raise. Laura remembers hearing her aunt say to a neighbor, 'I will look after Laura until she grows up.' Laura, hearing this, felt terrified of being left alone and thus decided not to grow up. She attempted to stay little and childlike as long as she could. Now in her marriage this is causing many problems, because Laura often gets sick and acts helpless in order to be taken care of by her husband and friends. She does not use her own Adult ego state very often to take care of herself or solve problems.

It is understandable that Laura felt terrified when she was three and needed to find a way to be cared for. As an adult she needed to grow up and be responsible. In therapy she did make a redecision to be responsible and use her Adult. She began to understand that her fear of abandonment came from her three-year-old feelings and was not reality now. As adults, people cannot be abandoned, they can only be left. This means that as adults people can leave us, and that may well hurt; but we can survive and take care of ourselves. A baby is abandoned because it cannot survive without someone to care for it.

Don't Succeed messages often come from insecure parents who do not feel confident themselves. A father with low self-esteem who did not finish high school may feel threatened and jealous when a son is intelligent and does well at university. On the surface father may act proud; however, the father may give a subtle message of, 'don't you think you are going to be better than me!' Father may feel jealous that his son is getting opportunities that he was never able to have. The son, if he obeys the Don't Succeed message, may go to university and do well in class, but then sabotage himself and not ever make it to graduation. This can lead to continuing failures.

Don't (do anything) was a message Diane got from her nervous mother, who feared that Diane would hurt herself with just about everything. Mother was frightened of Diane going swimming, riding a bike, climbing a tree, staying over at a friend's house, or just being far away from the home. Diane as a result became anxious about living and thought the world was a scary place. Diane became a nervous person who often felt anxious and had panic attacks. In therapy Diane discovered that the fears she felt were in reality her mother's fears and not hers. Diane decided in redecision work that she did not have to take on her mother's fears any longer, and that she was now going to enjoy life.

An interesting recent discovery from neuroscience has found that a parent's feeling state can be passed onto a child neurologically (J. Dispenza, 2007). This says that if parents are depressed, nervous, tense, scared, or angry and irritable, this can be passed to a child. Parents can pass those feelings to a child by modelling them as if to say, 'this is the way to feel in life,' as well as a child picking up parent's feelings from being in their vicinity.

I have worked with countless clients who have one or more of the above feelings, and do not understand why they feel that way because their lives are good. On exploration, we discovered that those feelings came from their parent. It was the parent's feeling state. The client could from this understanding then hand it back to the parent in therapy.

David was a shy young man who came to therapy wanting to gain confidence in himself. With script analysis work David remembered that his busy distant father rarely gave him much time or attention. If David attempted to talk to his Dad, he would get irritated and tell David to go away and not bother him. Understandably, David decided he was not important, and was a bother to people. In order to protect himself and get along with others as best he could, he decided to be quiet, not say much, and stay out of others' way. David went through school thinking he was not important or as worthwhile as others. I explained to David that in order for children to grow up to feel worthwhile, they need to have experienced being worthy of their parent's attention. David did decide that he was worthwhile and important using the therapy process of self-reparenting. I will talk more about this later.

Don't Belong is a message that is given to children that leads them to believe they are different from others. When children are teased at school for being from a different race or culture, or when parents scapegoat a child or tell them they are not as good as their siblings, children may decide they don't belong. For example 'What is wrong with you, Why can't you be like the other boys, you are not like us.' Then the child believes there is something wrong with himself and he feels inferior to others. Or, conversely, when children are told they are special and better than other children, this too causes problems. These children then believe they are better than others and have a superior attitude. As a result they have a hard time fitting in and making friends because friends don't tolerate well a person being arrogant and superior.

Ellie grew up with a Dad who was shy himself and who found it very hard to express his feelings. Ellie's Mum was often sad because Dad did not express that he loved her. Dad would say, ' I can't do that, it's the way I was brought up,' and thus he did not attempt to change. Ellie experienced that when she tried to get close to him by wanting to sit on his lap or have a hug, Dad was uncomfortable. Ellie decided she was a bother when she wanted affection and she decided not to be close, especially to men. Later in her relationship, she found it difficult to let her partner hug her, even though that was what she longed for.

Frank's father was a busy dedicated doctor and therefore always busy taking care of others. When Frank was little he discovered that when he was sick his father was then present and gave him attention by taking care of him, and when he was well, his father was back to taking care of others. So in order to get his Dad's attention Frank would often get sick. Throughout Frank's life he was often ill and did not understand why. When he remembered the early times with his Dad he then remembered making a decision at the age of five, 'I'll get sick again so Dad will take care of me'.

Lucy experienced that when she and her sister were down at the same time with Mumps, their mother seemed to be happy because she felt needed and important. Mother would talk to her sister and friends every day and obtain sympathy from them for having her girls sick. Lynn decided to please her mother by often being ill and allowing her mother to feel needed.

A different example of 'Don't be Well' can be seen with the life of George, who was a young athlete in high school. He was the star of the basketball team and the team and coach counted on him. One year he injured his back and could not play for a season. When he was recovering and slowly returning to play, the coach told him not to practise too hard; 'Save yourself for the game', said coach. George quickly found that the sore and injured back could be used as an excuse to get him out of things he didn't want to do. When asked to do something he could say, 'Sorry my back is playing up, I can't do that.' This became a pattern in his adult life, that his back would 'play up' whenever there was something George did not want to do.

The important reality of this process is that when a person creates this kind of thinking and invites illness or conditions to exist, then it can become the reality of what that person manifests in their life. The illness became real, not imagined. George did in fact have many operations on his back and the condition became worse. We need to be careful what we ask for.

Another example was an elderly person who was afraid her husband was going to leave her. She said to several people, 'If I was sick and couldn't take care of myself, he would have to stay.' Sure enough, she became very ill and her husband did stay and cared for her for many years. The illness became real, not imagined, and she eventually died from the illness that she had created. Our minds are very powerful and we create reality by the way we think.

'Don't Think' is given to children by belittling their efforts to think. When three year old Sue told her Dad she knew what five and five was, he teased her with, 'Well miss smarty pants, who do you think you are.' Sue decided it was better not to show that she could think. In addition, Sue's mother was a person who got upset and escalated feelings in order to get her needs met rather than think to solve a problem. So mother modelled that women don't need to think. As an adult Sue would act confused or upset when faced with a problem rather than think about a solution.

Ellie's father, in addition to being uncomfortable with her attempts to get close, also became very angry at her mother's expression of feelings such as sadness and anger. Ellie watched as her Dad became disgusted at Ellie's mother for showing feelings, therefore Ellie, wanting her Dad's love, decided to not show feelings and to be strong instead.

Below are some usual decisional results of injunctions.

INJUNCTIONS   POSSIBLE DECISIONS

Don't be …	I'll die and then you'll love me I'll get even if it kills me
Don't grow up …	OK. I'll stay little. (Non sexual – little girl voice)
Don't be a child ...	I won't ever ask for anything again I'll take care of myself I'll never do anything childish again I'll never have any fun
Don't make it ...	I'll never do anything right I'm stupid I'll never win I'll beat you if it kills me I'll show you if it kills me
Don't be close …	I'll never trust anyone again I'll never get close to anyone I'll never be sexual
Don't be well or sane..	I'll be sick I'm crazy
Don't be you …	I'll show them I'm as good as any boy/girl No matter how hard I try, I can't please them I'm really a girl with a penis – vice versa I'll pretend I'm a boy/girl
Don't be important …	No one ever lets me say or do anything No one listens to me –

Everyone else counts first around here

Don't belong ...   I'll never belong to anyone

Don't think ...   I'm stupid – I can't think for myself

Don't feel ...   Emotions are a waste of time
                  I don't feel anything

Don't feel that ...   I'll never let him make me cry again
                  I'll never show anger again
                  Anger is dangerous

Redecision therapy is based on the belief that:

'The individuals write their own script and can rewrite it with the help of a strong Parent ego state they build for themselves' (Gouldings, 1997).

    Remembering that it is the child who makes the decisions to obey or not obey messages that were given (often for good reasons of survival and to get along with scary grown ups), the good news about that process is that your Child ego state can change early decisions and put together a new program for living. All injunctions should actually be permissions. For healthy living the messages should be: It's OK to Exist, to Be You, to Be Childlike when you want, and to be Grown Up when you want. It's OK to succeed, to do new things and take risks. Everyone is important and it's OK to Belong, to Be Close and well and to use your thinking abilities. And certainly it's OK to express feelings.

    For myself I remember many times in my childhood when Mum worked on Saturdays and my sister and I were given the chores of cleaning the house and having dinner ready when she and Dad came home from work. If I did not get the tasks done when she got home, tired she became very angry and scary. I decided that I would always get the work done before I played. (That made sense at that time in my life to protect myself.) However, as

an adult, I had problems relaxing, or not being busy all the time doing work. That led to me being tired and often irritable when others
were not doing as much as I was doing. (They didn't have a chance
because I worked so hard and fast that no one could keep up, and
that made them feel inadequate around me.)

On the positive side it led to my career success, but on the
negative side it made me tired and created problems in my relationships with partner, children and friends. Sounds familiar? I have
now changed that early decision, and I don't work so hard, and I
give myself time to relax. I did this by telling my mother in my
head that, 'I am now a grown up, and I will choose when I work
and when I won't, and I am no longer scared of you because you
can't hurt me now'. That was very freeing for me. You can become
mindful of the times and situations where you feel uncomfortable,
and ask yourself, What does this remind me of from my childhood? When did I feel this before? You will then discover the early
scenes or times, and you can then make the changes you want to
make. Imagine being young, and from your Child ego state, tell the
person involved how you felt, what you decided, and what you are
going to do differently now. Because this needs to be done from
your Child ego state to be most effective, the process will probably
evoke some feelings, which is what you need; however, if you have
problems doing this, or feel too uncomfortable, stop, and find a Redecision TA therapist to help. You made the initial decisions when
you were a child, so to make your redecision most powerfully you
need to go back in time and become your Child ego state.

Sadly, in our culture many males have been told they are
sissies or girls if weak if they show feelings. This causes problems
and is of course unhealthy. For a start I feel it is discounting to
females to insinuate that we are bad or weak for showing feelings.
Secondly, medical science has shown that when people suppress
feelings of anger or sadness it often causes illness and or depression. It certainly adversely effects relationships when feelings are
not expressed. In my view it takes more courage to show feelings
and be transparent than it does to withhold them. Intimacy is risky,
but also incredibly rewarding when we take the risk.

In a relationship, when one or both partners hold in feelings and don't say what they are angry or frustrated about, a brick wall often develops. I call this the wall of trivia because many of the frustrations are small things, but when held in, one on top of the other, the wall becomes larger and difficult to deconstruct.

Imagine two people face to face with their Child ego states facing one another. Each time one person does not express a frustration, a brick gets added to the wall. The couple may think they are doing well to not fight, by stopping anger. Often couples say to me, with pride, 'We never fight.' However, when anger is blocked, then all feelings get blocked. The couple can feel the wall that has developed, and soon one or both start to feel that they no longer love the other. Passion, excitement, joy and sexual desire are also blocked. This leads to feeling the relationship is over. Often couples separate unless they un-block the wall by talking about their frustrations and angers, or issues they are sad about.

I have worked with hundreds of couples who come to therapy on the verge of divorce, where one or both state they don't feel they love the other anymore. When I describe the wall of trivia, they usually say, 'That's just how I feel.' I send them home to make a list of all the things they have been angry or frustrated about since they met. Big and little things. Many say, 'that is going to be a very long list.' When they come back with their lists, I sit them down facing each other and invite them to start talking and expressing their frustrations, one at a time. It is very important to take turns and listen and hear each other. Do not adopt an attitude of defense or get into, 'Well I did that because you did...' or, 'I would not have done that if you had ..... or had not....' That will lead to more anger and you will get stuck. You need to adopt an attitude of wanting to really hear and understand how the other person perceived the incident. How they felt about it, what it meant to them. Ask questions. How did you see that? What did that mean to you? How did you feel about that? You can also ask, Did that remind you of anything from your childhood?

Many times if not most times, things that upset us have some historical sore spot to them. That does not mean that your partner is not at all responsible for hurting you, but it does mean that if the sore spot from childhood was not there, then the incident might not have had an impact. A personal example from myself is that when my partner had his nose in a book and did not talk to me for hours I would get upset. After many fights, we talked about it and I remembered that as a child when Mum was angry at me, she did not speak to me for hours or days. I felt scared and unloved. I then transferred that onto my partner and felt the same when he was reading. Once we understood that, we could deal with it differently.

When you start talking about your list of frustrations it may seem daunting at first, but after talking about a few, the others will disappear. The important process of the talking is that you will connect to each other again. Most importantly, keep the intention of wanting to hear and understand each other. Cross the bridge to their mind and feelings, leaving yours behind until you have really heard your partner. Then they will cross the bridge to your feelings and perceptions. This is true loving and it will take you out of the power struggle. When you have connected to each other by talking to eye to eye and heart to heart, love will flow again, and problems will disappear. You will experience what many couples that I have worked with experience, that issues vanish when love is present. Maintaining connection by talking eye to eye and heart to heart on a regular basis, expressing feelings honestly and safely, is the best prescription for sustaining love. The walls can't survive in that atmosphere.

One other important way to keep love present is to make a commitment to do many caring loving behaviours to and for each other on a daily basis. As I talk about in Chapter three, giving strokes or warm fuzzies are most important. J. Gottman, a famous researcher of relationships, in his study of happy couples found that they did 100 caring behaviours for each other every day. A touch, a smile, listening, a stroke of appreciation, a hug, a cup of tea or coffee, etc. So many possible things, that costs little.

To start this practice, ask your partner to make a list of 20 things that complete the sentence: I feel cared and loved by you when you..........

This will tell you what they like, rather than giving what you would like. Often we miss our partner by not giving what they want. We tend to give what fits our script rather than theirs. Also give some surprises of things not on the list.

Exercise

If you would now like to get an idea of what script components of the Drivers and Injunctions you have, I invite you to do this exercise. If at any time it feels uncomfortable, stop, and perhaps take it to your therapist or counsellor or a friend to support you through it.

Think about a time when you were a child, but don't go to the most upsetting or scary scene. Pick one that is what you might call having a bad day. I want you to take care of yourself in this exercise and not go to anything that is overly upsetting. Any memory will do.

1. Think about when you were a child, what were the things that you knew you could do that pleased your Mum and Dad.

Mum was pleased with me when..
....
....
....
....
Dad was pleased with me when..
....
....
....

Examples:

I was being polite and helpful
I did things really well (like getting A's in school)
I kept trying and trying
Because I am strong and dependable
When I did thing quickly and was always punctual

What drivers do you feel they were giving you?

Drivers are:

Be Strong
Be Perfect
Try Hard
Please me (Please others)
Hurry Up
Work Hard
Be Good

Many people have all of the above or several of these, so write as many as you feel were present.

2. What was it about you that most upset or scared your Mother?
....
....
....
....
....
What was it about you that most upset or scared your Father?
....
....
....
....
....

Examples:

*Being irresponsible
(close)
Being independent
Being a girl instead of a boy
Looking the way you do
Moving away from home
Staying home too much
Asserting your opinions
Showing the feeling of...
Anger/fear/sadness
Insisting on your rights*

Being physical

*Doing risky things
Having fun
Being successful
Having been born
at all
Being strong and
healthy*

What do you feel they were telling you not to do? Usually not in overt words, but implied.

Think about a bad Day event that happened in your childhood, at home with parents and family, or perhaps at school or with older siblings. What was the situation that was occurring? Who was doing what? Who was saying what? What 'don't' messages were they giving you? What were they telling you not to do, or to do? What did you decide to do, or not do, to protect yourself? What did you need to do to get along with them?

....
....
....
....

Which of these injunctions did you feel they were giving you?

*Don't Exist
Don't Be You
Don't Be a Child
Don't Grow up
Don't Make it
Don't (Do anything)*

Don't Be Important
Don't Belong
Don't Be Close
Don't Be Well
Don't Think
Don't Feel

What were you feeling in each of these circumstances?
e.g. angry, sad, scared, ...
What was it that you wanted that you did not get?.........................
....
....
....

What did you decide about yourself, about others, and about life?

Self, I am..

Others are..

Life is..

How have these messages and decisions affected your life and
how are these decisions still affecting you in your life now?
....
....
....
....
....
....

What new decisions will you make now?.......................................
....
....
....
....

I suggest you imagine telling your parents or others of your new decisions. Imagine them one by one sitting in a chair in front of you, or draw a picture, and tell them the story of what happened and how you felt. Tell them what you decided at that time, and now tell them what you are deciding now that is healthier for you. Or write a letter and tell them. (You may not want to really send it). (Please do this safely by having a friend or partner there with you, or if you feel uncomfortable, take this to your therapist or counsellor.)

Imagine what their response would be, and how you will deal with that response.

Sometimes the parent response is supportive of new decisions, and they apologize for what happened earlier. At other times the message may still be the same from the person, saying again Don't........

It is important to think about what their response will be and how you will deal with it, because if you don't do that consciously, then it will rise up again unconsciously.

You might want to spend some time on writing about all this in a journal so that you can explore the details in depth, and get in touch with your feelings, and with what new decisions you want to make. Again, you may want to take this to your therapist or friend for support.

(Thanks to Jeff and Margaret White, and Bob and Mary Goulding for their contributions to script analysis.)

❦❦❦❦❦

Chapter Three
Strokes

A further Transactional Analysis concept that is important to understand, and that played a part in who we became, is the theory of strokes. There are four types of strokes, and as I describe them think about what types you received as a child.

Strokes are a unit of recognition, and can be either verbal or physical. A person can verbally say, hello, it's nice to see you, or physically give you a smile, hug or a touch. Children especially need recognition to survive and as adults we never outgrow this need. Berne talked about our human recognition hunger. For those of you who are parents, I'm sure you have noticed how children need attention, and if they are not getting positive attention they will act out, in order to get negative attention. Children and adults can survive on either positive (which of course is ideal) or negative attention. To be ignored and stroke-deprived is painful and damaging to one's psychological health.

Strokes can be:

Verbal or non-verbal   e.g. Hello (verbal) or a smile or hug (non-verbal).
Positive or negative   e.g. It' nice to see you (positive) or go away (negative).
Conditional or un-conditional. e.g. You did that well (conditional) or you are wonderful (un-conditional).

Being and Doing strokes. e.g. It's so nice you being here (being), or I like how you did ... (doing).

I explained above differences between verbal and non-verbal. I will now show other differences.

1. The first and best most health-producing stroke is positive un-conditional. This is a stroke for being, signifying that people do not have to do anything to earn this stroke. It is given simply for the person being present.

Examples are:

It's so good to see you.
I love your company.
The room lights up when you are here.
I'm so glad you are my son/daughter.
I love you.

These strokes build children's (and adult's) self-esteem. People on the receiving end of these decide, I am OK, lovable and loved. Unconditional positive strokes need to be given abundantly. I do not believe that children can be 'spoiled' by giving too many of these. The only way these can be a problem is if they are given in such a way as saying, 'You are *more* special than others, Others are not as good as you.' This may create a child who feels superior and arrogant. An additional caveat is to be careful with these strokes by not to giving them when a child or person is behaving badly. When there is bad behaviour parents need to say firmly, 'Your behaviour is not OK.' The message needs to be clear by saying 'It's your behaviour that is bad, not you personally.'

I have a fantasy or vision that I hold. If all people in the world were to start giving out more positive un-conditional strokes to each other, I believe the world would be healed and peace and love would permeate the world. I suggest you read Claude Steiner's book, *The Warm Fuzzy Tale*. It's a beautiful little book about the power of strokes.

2. The second stroke is the positive conditional stroke for doing. This is a stroke for complimenting or praising someone for what they have done well.

Examples are:

I like how you have cleaned your room, it looks nice.
I like the good grades you achieved this term.
You have done well with your sports, I like how you are playing well with your team.
Thank you for doing.......
You did a good job with that report/job.

These are useful strokes as they teach people how to do things well, and the person feels recognized and gratified. These encourage a person to develop and use their skills and strengths; gratification will be the result and the person will feel happy. However, if a child grows up receiving only, or mainly these, she will decide that the only time she is OK is when she is doing things, and doing things well or perfectly. She will probably become a person who is always doing, and find it hard to sit down and relax. (As I mentioned above, this was true for my childhood experience.)

Recent research indicates that if children are told, 'You are very smart,' too often, they may start to think they have to live up to that expectation, and may fear being seen to be less than smart at something. Those children may think they have to be perfect all the time. This may result in the child not being willing to try new things for fear of not doing well or not being perfect. It is better to encourage a child to try new things and give them permission to not do it well at first. Remind your child (and yourself), that in order to learn a new skill we have to do it badly several times before we become skilled at it.

The best strokes to give children, according to the new research, are specific conditional. For example, 'You scored well in that game,' rather than 'you were great.' This way the child knows exactly what he/she did that was good.

    3. Negative conditionals are also doing strokes. They are criticisms (hopefully constructive and given respectfully) for what the child or adult did not do so well.

Examples are:

Your room is not cleaned well, let me show you how it needs to be done.
Your grades are not good this term, let us work out how you can do better next term.
I don't like how you did this report, let me show you how I like it done.

    Strokes given this way illustrate to a person how things need to be done. The message needs to be, 'you are OK, it's only what you did that needs to improve.'

    As an opposite, examples which should not be used:

Your room is a mess, you are so useless at cleaning!
Your grades are bad, you are so stupid!
You made a mess of that report, you are incompetent!

    This criticism belittles a person and attacks their sense of being. These negative messages are damaging to self-esteem, and a child may well decide, 'I'm useless, stupid and I can't do anything right.' As he grows up he may be reluctant to do anything for fear of doing it wrong and being criticized again; or conversely, not being willing to do anything unless he is sure he can do it well. This creates problems, because for most people, we have to do things badly several times, we practise until we have learned to do something well. Who could drive, play a piano, cook, sew, ride a bike. etc. well the first time they did it? As mentioned above it takes making mistakes, and practise to perfect a skill.

4. Negative un-conditional strokes are destructive and hurtful and should never be given. They are negative strokes for being and personal attacks, giving negative messages that 'your being or who you are is not OK'. However, all of us, on a bad day or Mument, have said these, I'm sure, from time to time. If children are for the most part given positives   they can withstand the negatives occasionally. They will think, 'It's OK, I know she loves me, she is just having a bad day.' Ideally, when these are said, apologize as soon as possible.

Some examples of negative un-conditional strokes are:

You make me sick!
Get out of my sight!
I wish I had never had you!
Get lost!
Something is wrong with you!
I wish I could send you back.

These strokes destroy a childs' self-esteem. Children raised with repetitions of these may well grow up to feel suicidal. Those of you who may be youth workers, I'm sure will have experienced that young troubled people have had a history of being raised with these negative strokes.

If you are a person who was raised with many of these negative strokes, you need to know now that you are not bad, you are a lovable and valuable human being. The problem is with the person who gave you those strokes. It may well have been due to their own history. It was not your fault.

Children try different behaviours to test out which ones receive strokes or attention they want. The saying, 'what you stroke is what you get,' is true. If you give attention to positive behaviour you will get more of that. If you stroke negative behaviour, you will receive more acting out or bad behaviour. So, as parents, as much as possible, stroke what the child does well, and who they are, rather than criticizing the negative.

Strokes of course need to be genuine, not counterfeit. Examples of counterfeit are, 'The work you did was good, for a woman! That's a nice coat, did you get it at the second hand shop'? Some cultures have developed a habit of teasing, taking the mickey, bantering, putting others down, whatever you want to call it, and in my opinion it is very destructive and hurtful. The recipient may act as though they are fine and can take it, and give it back; however, I have had many men and women in therapy dealing with past hurts of being teased. Often the perpetrator when confronted will say, 'Can't you take a joke, I was only kidding.' The reality is that teasing and putting others down is not funny, it's hurtful. Let us work to create a culture where hurting, teasing, bullying, is not present.

Why do we have problems with giving positive strokes freely?

The Stroke Economy

Claude Steiner, psychiatrist and Transactional Analysis trainer, wrote some years ago about cultural negative rules. Many of us were raised with rules that result in us being careful giving out strokes, and accepting strokes.

These unhealthy rules are:

Don't give strokes when you have them to give.
Don't ask for strokes when you need them.
Don't accept strokes if you want them.
Don't reject strokes when you don't want them.
Don't give yourself strokes.

Adherence to these rules can cause many problems in relationships. In Imago therapy work with couples, one of the things I help people learn is how to give daily strokes or appreciations to each other. Most couples will say that two main problems in their relationship are poor communication and not enough positive compliments. It's usually males who do not give strokes or compliments enough because generally males were taught to be strong and tough, and told not to show feelings.

As a powerful way of improving your relationships I invite you to start giving out three to five positive strokes a day and watch the magic that happens. I guarantee things will improve, smiles and joy will be present. Remember to mix positive un-conditional strokes with positive conditional. I am often amazed that many people find it hard to give positive un-conditional strokes, the ones for people being who they are, saying what they value personality about others. Many have not learned how to give those because they did not receive them as children. Keep in mind that our parents often did not give positive strokes because they did not receive them from our grandparents.

E. Berne, as I mentioned earlier, spoke about humans' recognition hunger that is innate in all people. We need to be seen and recognized. We need to have a regular steady income of positive strokes to maintain our self-esteem, to feel good about ourselves, to know we are lovable and worthwhile.

Some people and organizations in our culture feel people who need strokes are 'too needy.' I have encountered this attitude when doing corporate work. Often supervisors or managers don't give positive strokes to employees, feeling employees are too 'needy' if they ask for positive recognition. This is a sad state of affairs. When employees don't get enough positive recognition at work it creates a loss of joy for work, it results in high absenteeism, poor team work, and a high level of people leaving. I believe that if everyone concentrated on giving positive strokes at work, to our peers, to people we manage or supervise, and to our supervisors, then joy for going to work would result. Imagine what it would feel like to say on Monday morning, 'Great, it's Monday, and I get to go to work and spend a day with the wonderful people at work.' What a change that would be!

Important point, employees; remember to give strokes upward too. Tell your boss, supervisor, manager, that you appreciate them. They also need recognition. 'Thanks for your support, for your help' would go a long way and takes very little time.

I believe in the context of evolution that we alive now are the ones that are moving up Maslow's hierarchy of needs, (I explain this later for those who may not be familiar with his work) and can now focus on self-esteem, belonging and self-actualization. Our parents and grandparents often still had to focus on basic needs of food and shelter, and therefore did not have time or knowledge to think about the higher levels. Our focus now has moved up to yearning for a spiritual connection of some description, of moving towards self-esteem and self-actualization. We can now learn skills to give and receive strokes freely. Receiving is just as important as giving. How many of us have been taught the Stroke Economy rule, Don't accept strokes? Messages like, 'Don't brag, You have tickets on yourself, You have a big head, Don't skite!' These result in people believing that they should not take strokes or need them. People learn to create what is called a stroke filter or shield, and thus not let positive strokes in. 'I didn't really do that well, it was nothing, I should have done it better, faster, you don't really know me, I'm really not that good!' If this has ever been true of you, learn to simply say, 'Thank you!' Learn to accept and take positive strokes in.

One of Eric Berne's often repeated sayings was, 'If you don't get enough strokes your spinal cord will shrivel up.' At that time, in the 60s, we thought his saying was a metaphor; however now with new advances in neuroscience we know that there is some literal truth to this. Healthy neuro networks and healthy psychological development are dependent on positive nurturing.

My wish and dream is that we all start to give and receive many positive strokes. If/when we do, the world will change. Start with our families, our partners, children, parents, siblings, relatives. We will then feel warm and loved, and connected. That will permeate to the rest of the world. Give strokes at work, in your community, whereever you can. One of the first things this focus does is change the way we look at people. We start to watch for what we like about people, what they are doing well, so that we can give genuine positive strokes. Our minds become more positive and less critical. Often we are focused on being aware of what we don't like, what is not going well, focused on the negative, being judgemental. As W. Dyer said, 'Change the way you look at things, and the things you see will change.' We could change the world, stop wars, by giving out positive strokes. Sound too far-fetched? I don't think so. We can give it a try it has to make an improvement.

Chapter Four
Existential Positions

All people, as Berne said, at around seven years of age, have made three very important existential decisions. These are a result of the above scripting processes, and from the types of strokes we have received. Other factors also played a part in these decisions. We have decided what we believe about ourselves, others and about our quality of life. These decisions are often held unconsciously or sub-consciously, and then what eventuates is that we repetitively manifest the same circumstances until we change those beliefs. You have probably noticed how the same kind of events or patterns keep happening over and over, and you seem to attract the same kind of people into your life. They repeat similar kinds of things that happened to you in childhood.

What we believe is what keeps showing up in our lives. This is actually the universe's gift to us. The situation is brought back to you, to give you the opportunity to change and heal from it. Each repetition is a chance to change an old decision. For example, if you have an old belief that 'all men are... or all women are... and they will treat me badly, then you will keep having that kind of person show up in your life. Change the belief to, 'there are wonderful men and women out there and I deserve to be loved and treated well'. A good and loving man or women will show up. You will attract through, the law of attraction, this kind of person. More about this later.

There are variations to beliefs we hold, and they can be

positive or negative. Let us return to the people we met in chapter 1.

Ann, who felt she had to be perfect in order to please her parents, but never achieved absolute perfection, because no one can, decided that:

Self... I'm not good enough, something is wrong with me. I'm not OK.

Others..are better than me. They are OK.

Life... is hard work.

Betty who had a violent and aggressive alcoholic father who beat her mother and at times the children, was often terrified. She became very watchful of Dad's moods and tried to keep him happy by pleasing him as best she could. She did this to protect not only herself, but also her mother and siblings. The decisions she made were:

Self... I have to make sure I please everyone in order to be safe. I am OK and capable of doing that. They need me. If I don't, something bad will happen. I might die or someone might be killed.

Others...(men) are scary and hurtful and can't be trusted.

Life ....is scary and unsafe. I have to be on guard all the time, especially around men.

Remember Bob who came home crying one day because he had been teased at school and his Dad got angry with him for crying and for letting the boys tease him? Dad told him he should always fight back. Bob decided:

Self...I am better than they are, I will always fight others because: I'm OK.

Others ...are not nice people and can't be trusted. They are not OK.

Life... is about getting others first.

You can imagine that Bob had problems at school and as an adult. He did not make friends, he was aggressive with others, and was arrogant and critical. These decisions, while they helped him survive when little by pleasing his Dad, did not help him as an adult.

Jill, who was the youngest of seven in her family and whose

mother tried to kill her when she was small, decided that;

Self....I am worthless and unlovable. There must be something very wrong with me. I'm not OK. If I can be helpful enough, maybe I can survive.

Others are... bad, and dangerous. They are not OK.

Life is....a struggle to survive and not worth it.

Jill was often suicidal, and whenever things went bad she felt she should kill herself. She did attempt several times but thankfully did not succeed. When she married, she found it very hard to believe in her husband's love. She would often sabotage things to make the relationship go bad, as she believed it always would in time.

She also, because of her decision that she needed to be helpful to be OK and survive, chose a career in the helping profession working with people in need. In her private life she attracted, unconsciously, needy and damaged friends that she tried to help and rescue. On one level this is admirable, but what happened later was that she burnt out and felt used. She was giving far too much time to rescuing others, and neglecting her partner and family, as well as herself.

Lynn decided;

Self... I'm a nuisance, something must be wrong with me. I'm not OK.

Others are...more important and better. They are loved. They are OK.

Life... if I can do enough (be better than others) then maybe I will be accepted.

Diane, who had the mother who was scared of life, and scared of letting Diane do anything that might be remotely dangerous, decided:

Self.... Life is dangerous, don't do anything risky. I'm not capable, thus not OK.

Others are...careless and stupid and do dangerous things. They are not OK.

Life is...scary, best not to do anything that might end badly.

George, who was the athlete who developed the back injury, decided:

Self...I am OK and important because they need me to win. I don't have to do anything I don't want to do. I am OK.

Others...are not as important as I am. They are not OK.

Life is....a never ending game for me to find ways to Not do what I don't want to do, and win at what I do want to do.

George, because of other events that happened in his life when he was small, also decided that people could not be trusted. He often was not comfortable around other people and his 'bad back' became a way of staying away from people.

Negative belief systems about self, such as, I'm not OK and there must be something wrong with me, result in what I call the 'flaw system'. Lynn believed, 'I must be flawed is some way. I don't know what it is, but there must be something that is not good about me.' Then Lynn feels she has to stay away from other people because she fears that if they get close to her then they will see the flaw and reject her and leave. So Lynn feels safer staying at a distance, not risking rejection. This is sad because the truth is that there is nothing wrong with Lynn and never has been. She has missed out on many friendships in life by staying away.

The opposite side is Bob, whom we met earlier. He decided he was OK and others were not. He decided to be strong and fight back in order to please his father. He had to see himself as better than others to survive with his father. Therefore he distanced himself from others, and treated others badly. He also lost out on having friends in life.

As adults, often, 'I'm not OK, You're OK' people, are attracted to 'I'm OK, You're not OK' people and form relationships together. The reason for this is a 'You're not OK' person likes to have someone to kick around so to speak, and put down so they can feel superior. It reinforces their beliefs of superiority. The 'I'm not OK' person feels they deserve to be kicked, discounted, and put down. They feel this is where they belong, and may accept this treatment for many years, which supports their old beliefs of being flawed in some way, until they change and decide they do not deserve to be treated abusively.

Once again, when these old beliefs are held unconsciously people want to prove they were right in that decision. The law of attraction is such that these will be the kind of people that will show up in their lives.

Many clients have asked, 'Why do I keep picking that kind of person?' That is why! The law of attraction, or the universe, what ever way you want to define it, gives us what we ask for unconsciously. Consciously a person may feel they are asking for a positive person or situation; however, the unconscious is very powerful, and if that belief is still present and lurking in the shadows, it may block the positive. So the answer is, find the old decisions and beliefs, and change them. This may take a little time and practice. If you are wondering what your old beliefs are, look at what is turning up in your life.

For myself, I remember when I became aware of old beliefs about money that came from my family. Messages from Mum and Dad were things like, 'Money is always scarce, and never enough. Rich people must have done something wrong to get it, Being rich is not who we are. Money is always a worry'; and so on and so on. You get the idea. Sound familiar to anyone? When I began to change these beliefs and used Redecision therapy, affirmations and EFT it took a couple of years to really clear the old beliefs. Then money started to flow much more freely in my life. Some old beliefs seem to hang around, and some changed immediately. I think it has to do with how strongly the old beliefs are held in the Parent or Child Ego state. Don't give up if you don't change things overnight- you can do it.

There is of course a positive possibility of existential positions which in reality is where we all belong. These are the confident people who decide:

Self.... I am OK, wonderful, capable, and lovable. I'm a good person and worthwhile.

Others are....OK and also lovable and worthwhile people. They are nice to be around and share love and life with.

Life is...Fantastic, fun, full of love, a journey to live and learn from, and share with others.

A person with these beliefs can create a wonderful life full of love and successes. Spiritually we are all one body and one consciousness, and thus all worthwhile and important.

The interesting thing about these and other script decisions in life is that we are stubborn people, and when we decide on something we want to prove that decision is right. Who wants to be wrong? Therefore we sabotage things, set things up to come out the way we thought. We can then say....'See I knew I was right, that has happened again, it always happens that way.' We keep manifesting the same thing over and over again. These decisions result in the diagram called the 'existential positions' or 'the OK Corral' developed by F. Ernst several years ago. As you can see the diagram shows the decisions about self, others, beliefs about quality of life, and how to manage life.

Existential Diagam F.Ernst

I'm OK - You're OK
Get on with others

High self-esteem
Non-judgemental
Accepts significance of self and
others
Confident, flexible
Open communication
Easy to talk to
Enjoys good health
Feels joy

I'm OK - You're not OK
Get rid of others

Triumphant, blaming

High regard for self
I've got rights, you don't
Demanding, critical
Pushy, bossy
Compettitive
Has 'Yes' people around
Suffers tension, stress

I'm not OK - You're OK
Get away from others

What's the point?

Low self-esteem
You have rights, I don't
Feels powerless, guilty
Does not feel comfortable with
other people
Is depressed, anxious, self-criti-
cal
Worries what others will think

I'm not OK - You're not OK
Get nowhere with others

Hopeless, Helpless

Low-self-esteem
I don't have rights, neither do you
My life is not worth anything,
neither is yours
Feels nothing matters
Blames the world
Feels desperate, vengeful
Resigned to unhappiness

Chapter Five
Rackets and the Racket System

I would like to start this section with an exercise. Think again of the event you wrote about above. What was the bad day event? What did you feel? 'Feeling' words are sad, mad, scared or happy. Not decision ideas such as, I was feeling that they were being mean to me. That is thinking rather than feeling.

Choose a feeling...

What happens with feelings and decisions is that we tend to choose a feeling during an early event from childhood and then we choose the same feeling when other events happen in life. We also, as I said earlier, want to prove the early decisions that we made, so in subsequent events, we stick to the same decisions. 'See, it's happened again, I'm worthless, stupid, no good. Others are better.' When things go bad, what is the usual feeling you get into? We tend to have a favourite bad feeling that we use in most situations. Many times the feeling we have chosen is one that was modeled to you by a parent or parent figure. We tend to use feelings that were modeled or encouraged in our family, and shut out feelings that were discouraged or prohibited.

For example, when things went bad my mother usually got sad, so I learned to get sad from watching her. We also choose feelings that work; feelings that gain our desired result. I remember clearly an early time in my life. I was about 4 years old and sitting at the dinner table. Dad got angry with me because I was not eating something. He made that angry growling sound that I didn't like and I got scared and froze. Tears were running down my face. Soon my Mum told me to get down and go sit on the couch. I did that and was sitting there feeling sorry for myself. Mum came and comforted me and gave me a hug. I remember deciding, 'So this is the way to get attention from Mum, to be sad and sulk, this works.'

I became a very good sulker until years later a dear Aunt who (I loved a great deal) and did not want to displease, saw me doing that to Mum, for probably the millionth time, and scolded me for my behaviour and told me to stop. I stopped sulking. Years later when I was well and truly an adult, I thanked her for doing that which got me out of my racket behaviour. She did not remember the incident, but I certainly did and was thankful.

So what feelings did you choose?

Remember Bob who was not allowed to feel sad or scared by his father, and had to choose to feel angry like his father in order to please him and survive. Lynn had to choose to feel happy all the time because father did not like sad or angry feelings. When children get scolded or ignored for feelings that parents don't like, they learn to suppress unacceptable feelings.

Feelings we choose are important to understand because they affect how we choose to live and play out our script. Additionally, keep in mind that staying in feelings does nothing towards solving the problems. People often tend to get addicted to feelings, believing they are the way we are supposed to feel, and assuming that if they stay in whatever feeling long enough, something or someone will change. It does not happen! Attempting to manipulate others by using feelings is game playing. It's better to be straight and honest.

I recently came across a saying that I think was a Sufi saying, and I don't remember the reference. The saying was something like...

'The bitterness I hold kills me, in the hope it will kill you.'

Holding onto feelings is a very unhealthy thing to do to

ourselves. Medical science is proving that to be true. It is believed that some cancers and heart diseases, and perhaps many other ill-nesses, may be caused by holding anger and bitterness. Don't do that to yourself.

We will again visit Lynn, who was often sad as a child because she felt unwanted as a girl and unloved; however, she had to keep the sad feelings shut off because Dad discounted her sad-ness. She became used to feeling sad internally and thought that was her normal state to be in. If things were going well in her life, she would often sabotage events to end up sad, or if there were no other people around to play her game she would tell herself sad stories internally. For example, she would imagine that someone had rejected her, so she could end up feeling sad and ill-treated.

Racketeering is the behaviour that a person enacts to set up or sabotage events to make situations turn out in such a way that the old racket feeling can be experienced. This feels familiar and comfortable, even though often negative. It often becomes addic-tive. This diagram illustrates what happens. People move from the calm happy state up the scale to the higher energies of sad, scare, and anger.

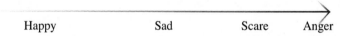

Happy   Sad   Scare   Anger

If children, for example, grow up in a household that has a great deal of anger occurring then they may come to believe this is normal and the way life is. The reality about anger, fear and sad-ness is that there is a certain level of excitement and high energy to those feelings. When people have experienced this level of excite-ment in life for years it can easily become addictive. Life can feel boring when things are calm and happy. I have often worked with clients with this addiction problem who say that when things are 'too quiet, too happy, too calm' they feel like they are going to die or disappear. These people become 'drama kings or queens' who create havoc to get an anger or sorrow fix. They will pick a fight, create a drama, or create a crisis. This process is usually done un-consciously. Their addiction becomes a part of who they are and these people will periodically sabotage life and events to create some kind of drama in order to feed their addiction. E. Tolle (2005) calls this our Pain Body.

This habitual pain body thrives on negative thinking as well as dramas in relationships. Once a person has created unhappiness and has been taken over by it, not only do they not want to end it, but they want to make others just as miserable as they are in order to feed their addiction. (Tolle, p. 145).

Racket feelings, therefore, are the habitual addictive feelings we choose to submerge into in most bad situations. We unconsciously set events up in order to again experience those feelings. It's like an old familiar coat, as I said earlier. It may be old and worn out, but it's comfortable and feels like 'me.' Racket feelings are also substitutes for real feelings in that, if a person experienced a feeling that was prohibited in childhood, then that feeling gets hidden and an acceptable feeling is substituted in its place. With Lynn, her Dad did not like to see sadness so she felt sad inside and became addicted to that, but only showed happy on the outside.

Fanita English, a Transactional Analysis trainer and writer, talked about authentic feelings versus racket feelings. Racket feelings are those feelings we use that we have learned to substitute for our real ones, feelings that were acceptable and modeled when we were young. Racket feelings are real at the time, but are a cover-up for underlying authentic feelings. Bob, for example had learned to show anger (that was acceptable to his Dad) instead of sadness for which his Dad condemned him.

We also learned racket feelings as children, according to what worked to get our needs met. Mary Goulding, co-founder of Redecision Therapy, often used the example, 'When you were little, what worked to get an ice cream if your parents said no at first?' If you asked for an ice cream, (or whatever you wanted) and they said no, what did you learn you could do that would win the ice cream? Could you cry, have a tantrum, beg, be very good and please them in some way, or perhaps sulk until they gave in? Are you still using that feeling and behaviour to get what you want? Perhaps you learned not to ask and became a victim, who believes

'No point in asking, I never get what I want.' Maybe that was true in childhood, however, things in the real world are different now. Ask straight for what you want. You have a much better chance of obtaining it, than if you don't ask. People are not mind readers.

When we learn a way that works as a child, we often continue to use that method as an adult. With our partners, if they don't do as we want, we feel sad, hurt or angry as we did as a child, and often access our reptilian brain and revert to childhood behaviours. Our reptilian brain is our 'old' brain that contains early memories and behaviours. As a hungry baby we cried to get our needs met. Therefore as adults, if our needs are not being met, we may revert to those early behaviours from our reptilian brain. We cry, get angry, make threats, have temper tantrums or sulk and withdraw. These behaviours are power plays, games, and do nothing towards solving problems in an adult way.

Expression of real feelings and making clear requests for change are much better ways to solve problems. When a person tells another in an Adult, straight, clear, safe, way, what they feel angry or sad about, and what they would like changed, then change is more likely to occur. Process of change and growth needs to occur in relationships. We actually unconsciously hired our partner to push our buttons and be difficult, because that brings up the issues from our past and gives us the opportunity to heal. I know that sounds a bit crazy, but none-the-less true. Sadly we usually don't know this, and instead of taking the opportunity to heal, we create power struggles with our partner.

The Celestine Prophecy (1993) talks about different roles that people manifest in order to take power from others, ways that humans compete and try to dominate each other. As children we often felt we had no power or that adults had more power, or we felt insecure. So we learned ways to gain power from others by taking on these different roles. Poor Me, Aloof, The Interrogator, or The Intimidator, are all roles the Celestine Prophecy speaks of, and they are similar to roles and games in Transactional Analysis theory, which I will talk more about below.

The **Poor me** role is taken by a person who chooses the

'victim' position. The purpose is often to gain sympathy, attention, be rescued, and taken care of by others. This person operates mostly out of Child ego state. Early beliefs that lead to this position are something like, 'I'm unlucky and useless, others have all the luck in life, life deals me one bad thing after another'. These beliefs held either consciously or unconsciously then cause blocks to creating a successful life. Negative beliefs are manifested repetitively throughout the person's life, until changed. Examples of what a Poor Me person might say are, 'I'm tired, That's just the way I am, I can't change, I'm doing the best I can.' This behaviour may well cause others to feel guilty. The inner struggle for a Poor Me person is often, 'I do so much, no one sees me, if I change no one will love me, no one cares about me, There must be something wrong with me, people treat me badly'.

Aloofness is a passive role taken to create distance initially, however the intent is a desire for someone to rescue them, to ask what is wrong, and thus they gain attention. Examples of what an Aloof person might say are, 'I need time to think about this, I'm not ready, I'll let you know.' This may make others feel uncertain and/or suspicious. The inner struggle for the aloof person is, 'I'm not sure I can survive, I'm afraid, I'll be trapped, I don't know what I feel.'

Interrogators are people who attack and interrogate others. 'Who do you think you are? Where do you think you are going? Why didn't you...?, Why don't you...?' This behaviour causes people to feel monitored, negated, and in the wrong. This outer behaviour is a facade of being superior; however the inner struggle is often, 'No one cared about me when I was a child, people leave me and I'm scared, I need proof of your love'.

The Intimidator, is aggressive and takes energy from others by intimidating. They often don't listen to others, are angry and arrogant. A 'me first' attitude, and they escalate into a rage easily and may get violent. Their attitude is one of 'get it any way I can'. Others feel scared and negated around them. Their inner struggle however is often a fear of being controlled, which is usually what happened to them as children, a fear of not being or having enough, feeling no one cares, and thinking they have to do it all alone. People using one or more of these roles come into relationship with people in other roles and then dramas and games are played out.

TA Roles

Fanita English, cited in *TA Today* by Stewart and Joines, (an excellent book to read if you want to learn more about Transactional Analysis), defines four roles that people sometimes adopt. From Child ego state there are roles of 'Helpless' and 'Bratty,' and they correlate to the 'Poor Me' role above from *Celestine Prophesy.* From Parent ego state there are roles of 'Helpful' and 'Bossy'. These have similarities to 'Interrogator' and 'Intimidator from above.'

Why do we take on these roles? There are several reasons which I will talk about in games; however, one of the main reasons is feeling we need to power-play to gain energy or attention from others. Humans are fields of energy and when we feel our energy is low we tend to think we need to gain it from others by way of using these roles to play games and take power from them. The reality is that we need to connect to universal energy. The East calls it chi, or in science we could say quantum energy, or the field of all possibilities. We will visit this in the sections on science and spirituality.

Script System from Transactional Analysis Theory

All the world's a stage,
And all the men and women
merely players;
They have their exits and their
entrances;
And one man in his time plays many parts,
His acts being seven ages.
(Shakespeare, As You Like It. 1599, Act.2, Scene 7).

The Script system was devised by Richard Erskine and Marilyn Zalcman (1979), both Transactional Analysts and renowned trainers. Their model shows how life-scripts are maintained and played out throughout life. The system is defined as a 'complex set of unconscious relational patterns based on psychological survival reactions, implicit experiential conclusions, and/or explicit decisions, made under stress, at any developmental age, that inhibit spontaneity and limit flexibility in problem solving, health maintenance and in relationships with people' (Personal communication April, 2008, Perth training workshop). Erskine and Zalcman won the Eric Berne Scientific Award for this theory.

When people are acting out their scripts they will be replaying the outdated or distorted beliefs that I talked about above beliefs about self, others, and life. These beliefs were adopted early in life as a way of surviving and explaining away unfinished feelings, or as a way of making sense of what was happening. Under stress or in a crisis, people necessarily make decisions to adapt in order to survive.

Think of the feelings you usually affect under stress. When something bad happens what do you usually feel? Scared, angry, or sad? Return to Lynn, who usually feels a mixture of sadness and fear when something bad happens. For Lynn, these feelings originated in her childhood. When she did something 'wrong', her mother got angry and ignored her for what seemed like days. Being shunned to Lynn felt like she would never be loved again, and thus she felt scared and sad. Get in touch, if you will, with the feeling you go to when bad things happen. Now ask yourself, when did I experience this feeling when I was little, or when was the first time I felt this? What was the situation? You might want to write about this in your journal. What was the memory and what age were you? In that scene, what did you decide about your self, others, and life? The same decisions as you wrote about above? This may be where it began.

You could also write about subsequent memories of times when you felt the same, and visited those beliefs again.

Ask yourself, what other events occurred in your life where you felt those same feelings and believed the same about self, others and life? Then ask yourself, what behaviour did I turn to in order to protect myself or survive that situation? What did I feel inside? What story did you I tell myself ? What conclusions did you make about this event? As you will see from the writing we tend to make a repetitive pattern to our scripts. Under stress we will go back to old feelings and beliefs, and reinforce our original scripts rather than seeing things in a new light, with new beliefs. We tend to use the same behaviour to protect ourselves rather than more productive ways of solving problems. When Lynn was a child and feeling sad and scared she decided to withdraw and stay away from others. She did her best to be good and please her mother. As an adult she was doing much the same, trying her best to be quiet around people and please them.

Defence mechanisms of withdrawing, running away, fighting back, crying, shutting down, or sulking, do nothing towards solving problems. Can you see a pattern for yourself? Do you tend to feel the same old feelings, go to the same beliefs, tell yourself the same story, and use the same behaviours? Don't feel bad about this; most all of us have done this at some point in our lives. The thing to do now is change the pattern.

Looking at this in more detail. Lynn usually feels sad and scared when something goes wrong. She then goes back to her old beliefs of Self: I'm not loved or wanted, something is wrong with me. Others don't like me or want me around. Life is hard and scary. The story she tells herself is that she is not as good as others, or, important. People don't like her company. She withdraws and stays away from people, saying nothing. She goes through life repeating this pattern over and over, missing out on much joy and love from being with others. She sabotages events and relationships by withdrawing and staying distant until the other person finally, in frustration leaves. She then says, 'See, no one loves me for long. They soon see how bad I am and leave.'

Bob, who we recall earlier basically feels superior, usually gets angry when something stressful happens, reverting to his beliefs of himself as being OK and others are idiots, bad, and not to be trusted. He pushes people away by his anger and aggression and gets rid of them. He believes life is hard, the only way to win is be one step ahead of others. He tells himself that he is one of the few in the world that can see what other people are really like. As a result he misses out on close loving relationships with others. He remains a loner.

Bob's mistrust of the world causes him to emit this energy outward, and what manifest for Bob are repeated situations that prove to Bob that the world is a scary place and not to be trusted. He often has his car and house broken into, and people treat him badly, because that is what he expects, and therefore what he attracts and manifests. He does not recognize that he is manifesting what he believes. Bob has been in several relationships in his life, but he keeps himself at a distance, and when his partner wants to get too close he will pick a fight, cause an argument; and soon the relationship ends. He can then say, 'See, this always happens to me, they pick on me, people can't be trusted, life is hard.' He is not aware of the part he plays in this; he blames his partners for the problems. People usually don't discern that beliefs and behaviours they use, based on their old core beliefs, project an energy that affects others and the universe, and creates the same reality happening over and over again. What we believe, think, and put 'out there' is what we will always get back.

If you want to make changes to your script system, that can be done with any part of your system. Changing just one aspect will in time change the whole system. For example simply changing your belief about self, in time will change the other aspects.

Let us look at how this works. When Lynn changed her core belief about herself to, 'I am OK and lovable, people like to be around me', she did not run away from people. She stayed in their company and thus people treated her differently. They were able to show her that they liked her. Lynn then began to enjoy life, and enjoy being with other people. She soon found a loving relationship and enjoyed life. Because Lynn had changed her belief about herself, she also changed her appearance and dress. She became confident and more attractive. By changing her belief about life to, 'Life is wonderful and my world is safe,' she manifested that into her reality.

♥♥♥♥♥♥

Chapter Six
How and why do we make the world be the same, over and over?

Every day of our lives events happen and problems arise that we have to deal with. How do I deal with this person? How do I drive to work safely? What do I say to my children, husband, and friends? Each time, we have two main options. We can deal with events using our grown up Adult ego state or we can resort to old patterns of script, and re-run old beliefs. As we know, many people tend to go into their script and see the world according to their decisions made as children.

Tolle (2005) explains how many people are identified with the voice in their heads. These people are not aware of this process, and think they are their thoughts, and become possessed by their mind. This is the egoic mind, and it wants to remain in their lives, so it attempts to maintain possession by telling them the same old stories. Egoic mind carries opinions, long-standing resentments, existential beliefs about self being better than or less than others, and beliefs about others being better than or less than self.

Discounting is part of the process of seeing or creating the same events to happen over and over again. Once these core beliefs of self, others and life are in place we then tend to see only what fits into those beliefs. We only attend to what reinforces those beliefs. Our frame of reference becomes fixed on what we expect to see. It feels safer to us to have our world be predictable, to be known, rather than new and different. This is how the ego continues to strengthen itself. We tend to feel more secure when we think we know what is going to happen, how others are going to be, rather than being in the here and now of a totally new Mument, and stepping into the unknown and allowing something new to manifest. We like to make life predictable rather than dealing with a new possibility. In reality, life could be exciting and more growth could occur if we were willing to step into the newness of each Mument. Something new could evolve. Some new learning and growth could emerge. However, we often limit ourselves by staying stuck in the past, and we use the process of discounting to do this. Complaining and discounting are two of ego's favorite strategies.

Discounting occurs in several areas and on different levels. People can believe that some aspect of self, others, or life is less than they are in reality. When people say to themselves, or others, 'I'm no good, I can't do that, I'm not lovable, something is wrong with me', they are discounting self. If a person says, 'They are bad, you can't do that, you are not capable, not to be trusted', then they are discounting others. And when people say, 'Life is hard, a struggle, and you can never get what you want or win', they are discounting life. Discounting begins in one's mind with a thought, and since we cannot mind-read others, discounting is not observable. If a person is thinking, 'You don't like me', we don't know that is what is going on in their mind, unless they say something or act out overtly.

Discounting is defined as 'unawarely ignoring information relevant to the solution of a problem' (Stewart & Joines, p. 173). For example, I might be talking to a friend on the phone and get a sense or feeling the person is distant or wanting to end the call. When I hang up, I may transfer an old story, 'She does not like me, I've done something wrong, she does not want to be my friend anymore'. This was something I decided from an event that happened when I was seven years old, when my best friend said she didn't want to play with me one day. The reality that day was that she was sick and didn't feel like playing. The reality with the friend on the phone may have been several things. She might have been busy, her children might have been needing something, she might have been on her way out the door. Could have been any number of things. However, through transference and discounting all other possibilities, I could go back into my old script pattern from when I was seven, and decide once again my same old beliefs. I end up feeling the same old sadness.

Going into script discounts other possibilities and is passive behaviour that does not solve problems. Rather than feeling sad and hurt, I could ask my friend, are you busy? Or the next day call her and ask what was happening for her at the time of my call. From existential positions that we decided on when little, we tend to hold onto beliefs and make the world fit those beliefs. We ignore other possibilities.

To have another look at the cases I have been presenting, Jill may have decided when she was little that she was OK, but that her mother was not OK since she tried to kill her. Jill may then go through life seeing all other people as not OK. Betty, who had the alcoholic violent father, may well have decided that she was OK, and that men are not OK. This of course will cause problems for her as an adult in relationships with partners. She may well see all men as not OK. She may be critical and angry at her partners, and thus not have happy loving relationships. Lynn on the other hand decided that she was not OK and that others were better, and she will likely go through life seeing only what fits that belief and discounting other events that would prove that belief wrong; or she may well sabotage situations to make them fit the old beliefs.

Discounting is done via grandiosity. This means that we discount through exaggeration of some event or reality. Blowing things up out of all proportion is a good description of this process. Betty, for example, says all men are bad rather than just her father. When people say, 'You always... you never...' they are being grandiose because those words are rarely true. If people say, 'Nothing ever works out for me, I never get anywhere', they may well be discounting the fact that in reality they have not taken the opportunities that were present in their lives to make things happen. Or they may not be willing to remember the many times when things did go well. As the saying says; never say never.

Changing just one old script belief will begin to break up negative neuro networks and create new synaptic connections, allowing new beliefs and behaviours to develop. From this point new positive experiences can begin to be manifested in life. Much more on this in the next sections.

Keep in mind: at each Mument in our lives, when faced with dealing with people or problems or just in everyday living, we have many options or possibilities. We can use our Adult ego state to solve problems and deal with life according to the here and now reality, or we can go into script and re-run the old patterns and behaviours. Going into script does not bring change and growth; rather, we will create the same patterns to happen over and over again.

> *If the structures of the human mind remain unchanged,*
> *we will always end up re-creating fundamentally the*
> *same world, the same evils, the same dysfunction.*
> *Tolle, p. 22*

Passivity

Being passive is another way to maintain old patterns and beliefs. There are four passive behaviours *(TA Today)*.

> *Doing Nothing*
> *Over-adaptation*
> *Agitation*
> *Incapacitation or violence*

Doing nothing is a person not doing what is expected of them, or not doing something to solve problems. For example when you ask a person to do something and they don't do it, or do it late, or wrong; and for the opposite of course, when you are asked to do something and don't do it. Children are often masters at this. Parents can ask children to do something, and they do not do it, or say...'Wait until...can I do it later? Often it does not get done or the parent decides to do it. Parents may set a pattern for the child to think, 'If I wait long enough Mum will do it.' This behaviour can well be the set-up of a game in relationships. A wife, for instance, asks her husband to do something, he does not do it and she asks again, and still nothing is done, and she asks again. Then he gets angry and calls her a 'nagging' wife. The 'uproar game' begins! I often explain to clients that the definition of 'nagging' is having to ask several times for something to be done. If it was done at the first or second request, then it would not be necessary to ask repeatedly.

Over-adaptation is when a person does too much to please other people, especially when they don't really want to do it, or when the other person should be doing it. For example Mum comes home from work and the kitchen has been left in a mess, while the teenagers are sitting watching TV. Mum says nothing and cleans the kitchen, while feeling irritated. Generally speaking, many women in our culture have been taught to please others, take care of others, put their needs and wants on the bottom of the list, rather than caring for themselves. I'm not suggesting that caring for others is bad, just that it needs to be in balance, and caring for self is also important.

When a person is feeling angry or irritated about doing something, I feel that is a good indication that the person is doing something they really don't want to be doing and perhaps they need to look at that. What changes can be made? There are of course times in life when we have to do things we don't want to do, but where possible things need to be negotiated. If you find yourself in a position of having to do something you really don't want to do, then when you can, do something nice for yourself. It helps.

When a person has a Please Me driver that I defined earlier, it is a good idea to change, To re-decide that, 'I don't have to please others all the time, 'It's OK to please myself some of the time'.

Another way over-adaptation occurs is when one person (A) has been doing nothing and (B) gets irritated. A will then, for a while, become nice and helpful, and do what is expected to calm B down, then A will go back to doing nothing. I call this the suck-up syndrome.

Agitation is when a person agitates by finger drumming, foot tapping, wriggling a leg, pacing, raising voice, rather than solving problems. This is often used as a way to get the other person to solve the problem. For example a wife might say to her husband (who is agitating because she asked him to do something), 'Settle down, it's OK, I will do it.' Other forms of agitation are nail biting, smoking, and compulsive eating. The person who agitates is doing this in order to entice the other person to do the task rather than doing it themselves, or to push the other person away.

Incapacitation and/or violence often comes after a period of agitation. If the agitating person (A) is not successful at getting (B) the other person to give in to him, or do what he wants, then he may incapacitate or get violent in order to make B do what he wants. Both genders can be the agitator. Remember the person I talked about earlier who decided that if she was sick enough her husband would have to stay and take care of her?, she did talk herself into getting sick, and it became real. George, who found that having a sore back allowed him to skip things he did not want to do, used another form of incapacitation. I'm not saying all illnesses are a form of incapacitation, but, if an illness becomes repetitive and is used to escape from something then it is likely a form of incapacitation. Getting drunk or drugged are incapacitations. These behaviours often force another person to take care of the drunk or drugged person, because they become incapable of caring for themselves.

Sam's mother did not have a good relationship with her husband, Sam's father. She became enmeshed with Sam and wanted him to stay at home with her and not grow up. Sam did live with her for many years. One year Sam met someone he wanted to move in with. When he told his mother about this she soon became ill with dizzy spells and heart problems and Sam decided he could not leave. People who disable themselves in some way are often incapacitating. It can be conscious or unconscious. It can be imagined or become real. It's my opinion that a person who uses incapacitation to manipulate situations or others risks becoming ill or incapacitated permanently.

Becoming violent is a passive behaviour because it is behaviour that is not focused on solving problems in an adult manner, but rather to control a situation, such as preventing another person from talking to them about their frustration. Domestic violence is an example. One person gets violent to control the other, preventing problem-solving discussion. The perpetrator pretends to be 'out of control' and says they can't stop their behaviour. This is not true of course. They can control the behaviour, (Gregory, 2004). When a person acts out their anger feelings by becoming violent rather than dealing with problems it is passive.

In these examples of discounting, one person is discounting their ability to use their Adult ego state and think through problems to find a resolution. The other person discounts their Child ego state by not allowing themselves to have needs and wants, and is most often focused on pleasing others.

Passive behaviours become present in a symbiotic relationship, where one person uses only their Parent and Adult ego states, and the other uses only their Child ego. Those in the Parent and Adult discount the other's abilities with their attitude of 'You need me, what would you do without me, you are not capable', validating and reinforcing their 'I'm OK, You're not OK position and allowing themselves to feel important and superior. Those in the Child ego state discount their own abilities and thus reinforce their 'I'm not OK, You're OK' position, and they feel inadequate.

Many people also discount themselves by the use of 'gallows' laughter. Gallows laughter is when a person laughs or smiles when making a statement about something unpleasant or unsafe about themselves. Example, 'I got drunk last night and nearly crashed my car, ha, ha, 'I'm so stupid I always mess things up, hee, hee. Gallows laughter indicates a person is in script. It can be dangerous, in that it can move a person towards suicide, accidents, or continuing to sabotage their life and manifest negative occurrences.

If a family member or friend is laughing or smiling at negative occurrences in their life, it may be appropriate, with care, to say, 'that's not funny, I would like you to take care of yourself.' This may be helpful in bringing them to an awareness of what they are doing, and realizing that they are important to you.

Levels of Discounting

Earlier we looked at the areas of discounting being, self, others and life. Next are levels of discounting. People can discount: *stimuli or existence, significance, change possibilities, or personal ability to change*. Discounting the stimuli or existence of a problem is the most severe, when a person does not acknowledge that a problem is present, for example when a smoker is out of breath and does not notice. Or when a parent does not hear a baby crying.

Next is the significance level. This is when a person knows there is a problem or situation happening, but does not define it as a problem. A common example is when a person takes drink or drugs to the point of being incapacitated, but does not see that it is a problem. Alcoholics or drug addicts are often in this position. They may get drunk or drugged several times a week and not see that it is causing problems in their relationships, at work, and with their health. At this level a smoker would say, 'Yes I know I am short of breath put I'm OK'.

To discount the change possibilities means that a person may see that a situation is occurring, and that it is a problem, but not see that problems can be solved. In the example of the smoker above, the smoker might say, 'Yes smoking is risky but once addicted that is it'. The alcoholic person might say, 'I'm an alcoholic and that's that, drinkers can't change'. At the level of personal abilities, the person may say, 'Others may be able to change, but I can't'. Discounting at the change levels is less severe and the person can change and become aware of the reality of the situation fairly easily.

A good example of this process is a person who smokes. At the first level of existence, the person my ignore the fact that smoking is dangerous to health, and say those reports are wrong. At the next level of significance he may say, 'Some may get cancer, but I won't'. Then at the other levels he may say, 'People can't stop smoking once the habit is there, or maybe others can, but I can't'.

Discounting at the options or personal options level is the least severe and can of course be changed. Rather than saying, 'nothing is going to change things', or, 'I can't change things,' look for all the options to make changes and put them into practice. It may involve getting past fears. When thinking about doing something new, or doing what you have always dreamed of doing, rather than saying, 'I'm too scared to do that,' say, 'I'm scared, and I'm going to do it anyway.' The best way I know to overcome fears is to do the fearful thing, and as you learn to do it, the fear will go. To say or think, 'I'll do that when I'm no longer scared', results in staying stuck. You need to feel the fear, recognize that the fear usually comes from some old childhood experience, talk to your inner Child and reassure her, give her a hug, tell her you will keep her safe, and then do what you want to do safely. Reaching our full potential means reaching past our known comfort zone. Whenever we do something new there is usually some fear or anxiety while we are learning. It can also be excitement. Feeling fearful of something new is normal, it's nature's way of keeping us safe. Babies are born with a fear of falling, so innate fears make us do things safely.

Keep in mind that usually when problems are not solved, some information about problems are being ignored, or some possible options to solving problems are not being considered or put into practice.

Exercise

If you would like to explore this theory for yourself, think of an unsolved problem in your life. What is it? Think of the types and levels of discounting you may have been using. Do you see the problem as important? What have you tried so far? What have you not done, and why? What could you now do? Write below or in your journal about this.

❦❦❦

Chapter Seven
Symbiosis

An interesting but sad type of relationship occurs from using discounting and passive behaviours when two people behave as though they are one. Typically, as I mentioned above, one person will only use their Parent and Adult ego states and the other person will use only their Child ego state. Together they use three ego states instead of six. This occurs because of scripts.

Let us take another look at Betty and Frank. Betty decided that she was OK and that she was the responsible one in the family who had to keep it all together. She had to watch her Dad carefully and keep him from being hurtful, so she decided that men were not to be trusted and they were not OK. She also received many strokes from her Mum and siblings for the way she helped and took care of them. She became addicted to being needed. Her survival decision was to hurry up and grow up, and be responsible.

Frank, who as a child was often sick to get attention, and also often angry because of his parents being unavailable, decided the best way for him to survive was to stay little in order to be taken care of. When he was sick he was successful at gaining attention from them.

Betty and Frank were attracted to each other (largely because of the childhood images that they saw in each other) and married. Frank was similar to Betty's Dad in that he was irresponsible and childlike. He needed to be taken care of, and Betty felt needed by him. Betty was like Frank's parents in that she was over- responsible and often out taking care of others as Frank's doctor father had done. Betty was in Parent and Adult taking care of Frank, the house, their children, being the responsible one. Frank stayed in Child ego and was happy to be taken care of and left the responsibilities to Betty.

We are attracted to people who carry traits similar to our parents, especially the negative ones. Why on earth would we do that, you might ask? It is the way nature intended; it is about growth. Firstly, when we meet a person we're attracted to we may feel 'I have known this person all my life.' We have...they are our parents. Secondly, we are attracted to a person like Mum and Dad because our Child ego state is still trying to get some needs met that were not met in childhood. A person like Betty needed to have more physical strokes, more hugs and kisses. She was not given enough as a child. The irrational part of her Child ego state decided that it would be good to find a person like Mum and Dad, (who did not give many hugs and kisses), and then find a way to get that person to meet her needs. Then armed with that solution, she could go back and make Mum and Dad do it as well. This of course is totally irrational. We can't go back and make changes in the past. Even if Mum and Dad changed in the present, it would still not meet the needs from the past.

So...Betty was attracted to Frank because he was not good at giving strokes. He wanted to receive them but not give them. Frank was attracted to Betty because he wanted her attention and understanding, which he did not receive from his parents, but Betty was too busy caring for others, and angry that Frank was not meeting her needs. Frank was angry that Betty was not giving him attention, and he often became violent and abusive. They were stuck in a power struggle.

Betty used her Parent and Adult ego state to keep the house and family functioning. She took care of the bills, the housekeeping and raising the children. She felt like Frank was another child. This situation allowed her to feel indispensable and met her addiction of needing to feel needed. Frank remained in his Child ego state and was often sick, drunk or angry to get attention. He thought, 'If I make enough noise or am incapacitated she will have to look after me.'

The way passive behaviours were played out occurred when Betty asked Frank to do something, and most of the time he did nothing. Betty usually finally did things herself, while thinking, 'See I have to do everything, what would they do without me?' She became a martyr. If she got angry at Frank, he for a little while would over-adapt and do just enough to calm Betty down, then go back to doing nothing. If Betty pushed too hard for Frank to do things to help he would firstly agitate by getting upset and anxious, which usually resulted in Betty saying, 'Calm down, I'll do it.' However, at times when the fights escalated and got worse, Frank would either get sick again or get violent to stop Betty from pressuring him.

At the unconscious level both Betty and Frank are playing a part in keeping this symbiosis going. Betty discounts Frank's ability to think and be responsible and thus use his Parent and Adult ego states. Underneath she relishes feeling needed and she enjoys strokes from others for doing that. Many of her friends say, 'Betty you are wonderful for what you do and put up with.' So Betty as well uses the passive behaviours in that she does nothing about caring for herself, and nothing about really solving the problems with Frank. She over-adapts by being the 'useful' one. She also at times agitates by getting angry at Frank, but does not follow through with really solving the problems. Betty pushes herself to do everything and often reaches a burnout stage which, I believe, is a form of incapacitation, and a degree of violence to herself. At this point she has to slow down and not do so much, and she thinks 'Poor me, no one ever thinks of me'.

Betty and Frank are stuck in using their old defence mechanisms to survive and get their needs met, but it is not working. The way Betty survived in her family was to get busy and take control. The way Frank survived was to stay little and needy.

This couple will benefit from Imago therapy to learn ways

to get through the power struggles. All people are supposed to have the full function of four capacities. These are:

Thinking

Doing

Feeling

Sensing

Usually, because of parental script messages, people have had to suppress one or two of those in order to survive, and tend to over-develop the others.

For example, Betty, in order to survive learned to shut down her feelings; it was too painful to feel. She also learned to only think about what needed to be done to keep things together, not think about the problems that she rightly, as a child, could not fix, and not to think about what she wanted or needed. She became an over-doer, hypervigilant in sensing what moods others were in and what she needed to do to take care of the situation. She denied what she needed or felt because she was often told by her mother that asking for things was selfish and impolite.

Frank, in order to survive, shut off doing because he wanted to stay little and be taken care of. He suppressed sensing because it was painful when his parents were not around much. He used his feeling aspect to feel sick and be taken care of, and he used think-ing to think about how to get cared for. He did not think about his responsibilities and what needed to be done.

Betty and Frank are opposite in what traits they are using and, of course, opposites attract. Betty at first loved Frank's ability to be in his Child ego state, and she thought he was fun. He often did what he wanted to do and was good at self indulgence. Betty did not know how to do that for herself, but was excited at watch-ing Frank do that, and thought she could learn from him (which is exactly what she needs to do). Frank loved Betty's' sense of re-sponsibility and her efficiency. Later of course, Betty became angry at Frank for being 'a child all the time and not responsible'. Frank became angry with Betty for always being busy doing things and not having fun with him.

Betty and Frank must learn what their un-met needs from

childhood were, and then be willing to stretch and meet those needs for each other. Frank needs to learn to give Betty hugs and loving, thus to use his thinking to think about Bettys' needs rather than only his own. He needs to also use his feelings to compassionately give Betty love and physical touch and strokes, for her to just 'be' rather than be doing all the time. And he needs to use his thinking to be a responsible adult, and take his place in their partnership at managing the house, children and life.

Betty needs to use her feelings and thinking to give Frank quality time to be with him, to let herself have fun time with Frank. She needs to think about ways to relax, and not always to be doing things and being absent.

The spiritual gifts for Betty and Frank when they do this are that they will become whole people by bringing back to life their lost functions. They will heal each other in the process. What could be better? They will then have reached the final stage of relationship, true love.

The different symbiotic relationship positions can be taken by either the male or female, or in same sex relationships, by either person. Either can be the Parent and Adult and either can be in the Child ego state. An example of the other way is the fairly typical relationship where the male is the Parent and Adult strong silent type, keeping his feelings and sensing well hidden and shut down. He takes care of all the decisions, and the finances. She takes the Child position of being the person who works hard to please him, and takes care of the house and children. She says to

male

Nurturing Parent
Critical Parent

Adult

Free Child
Conforming
Child
Rebelious Child

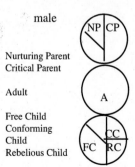

Messages from parents or parent figues cause children to shut down parts of their ego functioning.

female

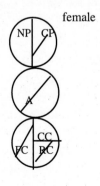

her friends that she likes a strong man to lean on, and in difficulties she dissolves in tears and acts helpless, leaving him to sort things out. She discounts her Parent and Adult ego states, and he discounts his Child. They are both getting their needs met of being needed, albeit unhealthily. Couples can maintain this relationship for many years...until one or both get frustrated with it.

We can look at this typical cultural-based relationship using the ego states in a more detailed way. This is generally speaking, and I feel was more true of our parents and grandparents, than now. I do see some couples, however, who are still in these positions (see diagram page 83).

Males and females who were raised hearing the traditional rules for how mothers and fathers, or husbands and wives, 'should be' develop the following type of relationship.

In this construct men have been told to be strong, in control, don't show feelings (except anger), be a man, Don't be a 'girl.' Think to be a problem solver, and have fun with your mates. Women are to have sex with, not be friends with. Boys will be boys, so being rebellious is OK. Being soft and caring is not manly. Total Free Child fun is not OK as it is too wild. You have to be responsible, do the right thing and provide for your family. Using the TA model of Functional Ego states, the result of these messages are that men develop their Critical Parent, Adult, Conforming Child and Rebellious Child. Their Nurturing Parent and Free Child are shut down.

Women, on the other hand, have been told, 'act helpless, boys like that, don't think, boys don't like that. You can show sad feelings but not anger. That is not 'ladylike'. Take care of others and be the nurturer and please others at all costs. Forget about your own needs, you will be selfish if you want things.' Free Child fun is certainly not OK, it is too wild. From these messages, women develop their Nurturing Parent and Conforming Child; they discount and shut down their Critical Parent, Adult, Free Child, and Rebellious Child.

So what happens when our above couple form a relationship? The only ego state in common that they have available is their Conforming Child (CC). This means they can talk about the children, the chores, the family schedule. He does the 'boy' jobs, she does the 'girl' jobs.

For adult conversation he talks to other men, because her Adult is shut down, she nurtures him, but gets nothing back from him. He is rebellious at times and spends time with his mates; she gains closeness from her girl friends, but not from him. They have sex but it is not really intimate. Neither one has real Free Child fun together. Real Intimacy such as talking about their feelings or their relationship is absent. A sad state indeed. I know this description may be exaggerated for current trends in our society; and it has changed a great deal over the years with women's liberation, but at times I still see young couples in these positions.

There are four stages of relationships. E. Bader and P. Pearson, (*In Quest of the Mythical Mate,* 1988) developed a model for understanding stages that relationships go through. They developed this model from M. Mahler's model of development, illustrating that the stages of relationship in many ways mirror the stages of child development (Diagram page 86).

Each circle represents one person in the relationship, represented by the box. Before forming a relationship people are separate individuals they are two 'I's'. Then as they form the relationship they become 'we'. From this point the 'I' and the 'we' fluctuate due to the struggle between the need for autonomy and the need for intimacy.

The first stage is Symbiosis (#1), and in the beginning of a relationship this is normal for the first 9 - 12 months. This is the romantic (H. Hendrix) or falling in love stage. Remember back if you will, the first time you met someone and you started falling in love. You wanted to be with this person every minute of every day. They were perfect and had no faults. Sex was amazing, and the rest of the world did not matter, you just wanted to be together. Differences are minimized and similarities are maximized. 'We are so much alike, we like the same things.' H. Hendrix calls this 'nature's narcotic.' Didn't we all love it? It is wonderful and perhaps the best feeling in the world. We need this stage because it bonds us. During this stage we get married or make a commitment, buy a house, have children perhaps, and acquire debts.

These bonds are helpful because when the stage of disillusionment sets in, the bonds keep us together. Not always, but at least for longer. Because of the bonds it is not so easy to walk out. The romantic symbiotic stage is not supposed to last forever (as much as we would like it to, and as much as it feels good, it is not real love or healthy growth). Many couples do stay in this for years and it results in enmeshment.

Movement to the second stage which is called Differentiation (#2), comes about when one person starts to feel smothered or too close to their partner. Sometimes life brings on this stage. Situations such as needing to be away for work, or having children

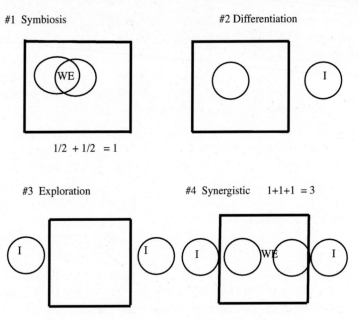

E. Bader & P. Pearson, 1988.

and the demands they make taking time away from each other. Differentiation begins when one person starts to put more attention on other things rather than their partner. That person, starts to say things like, 'I'm going out with *my* friends' and, 'No I don't want you to come. We don't have to do *everything* together'. Or, 'I have to travel for work, and, no, you can't come'.

This usually comes on the heels of the time in a relationship when we start to see our partner more objectively. They are no longer perfect with no faults. How did we miss those things at first? Remember that? He or she suddenly becomes human with human faults, and is no longer the God or Goddess! Some start to wonder if the relationship is really right. Is this really my soul mate?

This stage causes problems for many couples if they don't understand it. A desire for more independence or for some more personal space becomes an issue. The other may still want the symbiosis. When differentiation starts to enter a relationship, one partner is usually threatened and resistant to the changes. He or she attempts to cling to past closeness and this tends to drive a wedge further. They may well start to question if they still love each other, thinking maybe they should leave and start over. Many couples do leave a relationship during this stage. This is why bonds are important to hold it together. Many fights occur, or they try to solve problems by denying the differences and not saying anything. Thus the walls of trivia start to form.

What needs to happen in this stage is for both partners to develop some independent things to do Whatever that may be; work, sports, hobbies, friends, study, or another interest. This creates more interesting things for the couple to talk about when they do get together. When people spend all their time with each other they run out of things to talk about and the relationship suffers and can become boring.

The third stage is called Exploration or Practising. (#3) This is when the two are growing to be different independent people rather than the one 'we-ness'. In this stage one or both are more focused on their own life, their own self-esteem, than on the relationship. One or both may be more committed to study, hobbies, career, or parenting rather than on their partner. If both are in this stage at the same time it can feel like two ships passing in the night. Not much togetherness. If only one of the couple is here, and the other still wants the closeness, then one tends to cling, while the other takes distance: a real crisis time if they don't understand what is happening. It feels like love and caring have all but disappeared. They don't feel needed or wanted anymore. Complaints from this stage are often: I am on the bottom of your list, I'm not important to you anymore, You only think of yourself and what you want, You never want to spend time with me. Separation or affairs often happen during this stage, especially if one person likes to be 'needed'. They may try to find another person who 'needs' them.

If the couple commits to stay together and work through this time they can reach the stage of Re-Connection or Rapprochement. In this stage one or both have re-established their own identity and gained back some independence. They honour their differences and can discuss them without hostility. In fact they may well find that putting both views or ideas together creates a better situation than either one of them thought was possible on their own. A sense of being in a wholistic relationship starts to emerge. It is a different kind of 'we-ness' than before. Each persons' independence is honored. A deeper sustainable intimacy also develops, along with a renewed sexual relationship. The two separate 'I's' are respected.

This evolves into the stage of Synergistic relationship (#4) where the sum of the whole is more than the two parts. It becomes 1 person, plus 1 relationship, plus 1 person = 3, rather than the first symbiotic stage where it was 1/2 a person, + 1/2 person, = 1.

This stage has a spiritual quality to it, in that the couple feel fulfilled and grateful for their blessings. They often combine their talents in some way so that they create something for society that they could not do on their own. It is mutual interdependence. Intimacy deepens further. Both become who they really are in their identity, in their soul, and they reach their full potential.

This growth and achievement is certainly worth waiting and working for. It is one of the true gifts of life. The important fact to know about these stages is that we all have to go through them. I don't believe we have evolved enough yet, or are meant, to go immediately to the last stage. The growth along the way is essential. If people leave a relationship during the difficult stages of Differentiation or Exploration and then get into another relationship, they are still going to have to learn and struggle through those stages with the new partner. It is much cheaper and easier to do the growth with one partner, rather than with two or more. Having said that, the work does require both people to be committed. They don't always reach the point of being willing to do that at the same time. Many couples I have counselled have initial anger to deal with about timing. One will often say, 'I'm so angry that it has taken you so long to be willing to do this work, I asked you several years ago to do it, now may be too late.' It's usually not too late.

One factor I will say here is that if there is violence or abuse in a relationship, it may not be healthy to stay in these circumstances, unless there is real commitment to change. Domestic violence is an important and separate issue that needs to be dealt with skillfully in different ways (Gregory, 2005).

Often couples ask me, How long does it take to move through these stages?' In my experience, the first three stages can last for varying times, and people do not move from one to the other in a clear progression. There may be a merry dance of back and forth, and from one partner to the other taking the positions. Some couples never reach the final stage, some couples stay in the Symbiosis for sixty plus years. For myself, we have been married for forty plus years, and for the majority of time we have been in the fourth stage. What I do experience, which is heartening, is younger couples seem to move through the stages quicker. I think it has to do with a speed-up of evolution or spirituality consciousness.

Exercise on Passive Behaviours.

Think of times in your life and in your relationships that you have used (*being honest helps*) or the person you are in relationship with has used any of the 4 passive behaviours.

> *Doing Nothing*
> *Over-Adaptation*
> *Agitation*
> *Incapacitation/ and/or Violence*

Write in your journal about these times.

What will you do differently now?

....

....

....

ꣳꣳꣳ

Chapter Eight
Games

Most dabblers in the relationship circus have heard of Eric Berne's book, *Games People Play* (1964). It was a best seller for many years. Games are psychological processes that we all have participated in at some point in our lives. Have you and another person had an interaction after which you both ended up feeling bad? Have you had times with another person when something starts to happen, and you say or think, 'here we go again'? It is pretty certain at those times you were involved in a game.

What are games?

Games tend to be repetitive. When similar things happen over and over in life, it may well be because you or the other person are setting the same situation up time and time again. Games are played unconsciously, and as E. Tolle points out (2005) the purpose is to strengthen our ego. It's often not until the end of games that you may think, 'How did that happen again?' At that Mument there is some sense of being aware of the charade. Games always end up in bad feelings. Remember those feelings I talked about earlier? Feelings we learned from childhood that either worked to get you what you wanted, or were feelings that were acceptable in your family, or feelings that became your habit to adopt when things went wrong. For example, as I disclosed earlier, when things went wrong I used to always feel sad. Games occur from an exchange of ulterior communication. On the surface it seems OK but there is a sense of something else going on underneath. Some hidden message or agenda.

Looking at a common situation, wife says to her husband as he walks out the door for work in the morning, 'Will you pick up the cleaning today?' She knows he has a busy day, and lots on his mind. She thinks to herself...' I bet he will forget, he always forgets.' That night when he gets home she asks 'innocently'... 'Did you get the cleaning?' He says...'No, sorry I forgot.' Then the fight starts. This scene happens over and over again. They fight and they both end up in bad feelings. He feels guilty, she feels hurt but also triumphant that she has proved once again that men can't be trusted, which is a belief she took on early in life because of her father.

She goes through life setting things up to prove that men are bad and can't be trusted. Her position is I'm OK, You're not OK. He decided he was bad and stupid early in life because of being teased at school, and guilty when he didn't please Mum and Dad. He goes through life forgetting things and then says...'see, I'm stupid, I'm not OK'. Games always have a Mument of surprise or confusion 'How did this happen again?' People play games to validate their existential position. They use others to re-prove, over and over, I'm OK, or I'm not OK, and You are OK, or Not OK. Our partners are usually who we play games with over many years; however, we often use friends, other relatives, and work colleagues. The couple above could change this scene by doing something different. She could ring him later in the day to remind him, and/or he could make himself a note.

Exercise

Think of a painful time in your life. What happened and how did it end? Did it have any of the features listed above? Is this a repetitive pattern? What could you do differently to change the situation?

Games are played at different degrees. A first-degree game

is not so serious and people don't get hurt, usually. It is socially acceptable interactions, perhaps flirting at a party, or teasing other people in a playful way.

A second-degree game is more serious, and the players don't want others to know. It's behind-closed-doors interaction: fights, affairs, secret drinking or drug abuse, gambling, secret spending, gossiping. These games have heavier outcomes, and can end in severe fights, creating problems in relationships.

Third-degree games are very severe and as E. Berne described they are played 'for keeps.' The games can end up in morgues, courtrooms, or hospitals. For example, the game above with wife and husband arguing about the cleaning not being picked up could stop at the first-degree level with both of them laughing about the cleaning and dropping the situation there. However, if they escalate into a fight they move to second-degree. If they keep the fight going to the point of domestic violence, it can end up in the hospital and courtroom, or morgue.

The Game Triangle

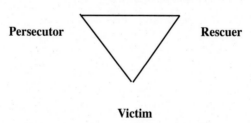

Persecutor   Rescuer

Victim

There are three positions in game playing: The Victim, Persecutor, and Rescuer. Steve Karpman, a TA trainer, (*TA Today*, 1987) devised this theory of roles. Persecutor is a person who is in I'm OK, You're Not OK position and likes to put others down, discount, criticise, and end up feeling superior. This position is usually a facade as the person does not really feel OK. If they really believed they were OK they would be in the I'm OK, You're OK position, and know that all people are equal, and therefore not play games. They instead see the world in a hierarchy of levels.

They don't feel they are on top, which upsets them, so they console themselves by thinking...'At least I'm not on the bottom.' To reinforce this belief they have to make sure there are people on the bottom that they can feel superior to. To maintain their superior position they discount, belittle, and put down vulnerable people in order to keep them on the bottom. Women, children, other races and cultures, and marginalized people they position as being 'different' from themselves are the usual victims. Some persecutor game labels that were named by Berne and have been used over the years by TA practitioners are, NIGYSOB, (Now I've got you, you son-of-a-bitch), Corner, (Got you trapped in a corner), and If it Weren't For you.

The Victim position is taken by people in the I'm Not OK, You're OK position. They mistakenly believe they are inferior in some way, and think they deserve to be on the bottom, put down and discounted. They allow themselves to be mistreated. Being a Victim allows them to maintain their script belief of, 'See, there is something wrong with me'. Typical games Victims play are: Poor Me, Ain't it Awful, and Blemish. As you can see, Persecutors and Victims fit together, and they often find each other to play games with. Persecutors like to kick others around, and Victims feel they deserve to be kicked, and consequently keep allowing the abuse to happen to them.

Rescuers also see themselves as I'm OK, You're not OK. They feel they need to help others, they feel superior, and enjoy being needed. Their belief is, 'I have to help because they are not good or capable of helping themselves.' I also believe that some rescuers can be in the I'm not OK position thinking, 'If I can be helpful enough to you, you will think I'm OK.' Rescuers will do things for people without being asked. They swoop in like knights in shining armor, and do things for people, often causing others to feel inadequate. Rescuers will also rescue victim people who love being taken care of; the people who play helpless to invite rescuers to help. This allows Victims to stay Victims. Typical games rescuers play are, What would you do without me?,   I'm only trying to help. If you feel you are a rescuer, I offer two rules to follow to stop that behaviour.

Rule 1. Don't do things for others unless they ask you. This does not mean that you stop helping or caring, but it does mean that you invite others to ask. Instead of jumping in, taking over, and helping too much, ask the other person, 'Would you like a hand with this? I have some extra time, do you want me to help?' In extreme situations of course we rescue without being asked, such as when a person is in a burning house, or drowning, or having a heart attack. But in day to day events, it is best to invite the person to ask for help. To do it without allowing them to ask can cause them to feel inadequate. It sends a message of you not thinking they are capable of doing whatever the task is.

Rule 2. Don't repeatedly do things for others that they are capable of doing for themselves. What I mean by this is that Victims will play helpless, and ask and ask, and if a rescuer keeps helping it allows victims to stay victims. It is better to say, 'No, I don't want to take the opportunity away from you to learn how to do that. I know you are capable of doing it. You need to do that yourself.'

With game positions of Persecutor, Victim and Rescuer, we can switch from one position to the others, sometimes very rapidly. A person can start a game in Persecutor position, such as being critical of the other, then when the fight starts person A will switch to Victim, and say, 'Poor me, I always end up the hurt one.' Or a Rescuer can start a game by saying, 'Let me help you,' and then switch to Persecutor when the other person does not appreciate her help, or do what is suggested. A typical game of this type of interaction is called, Yes But. Rescuer offers solutions to a problem to a Victim, and to all the suggestions, the Victim says, 'Yes but that won't work because...' The Rescuer after several suggestions becomes frustrated and moves to the Persecutor position, and will then criticize Victim by saying, 'you are hopeless, you will never change.' The Victim can then move to Persecutor and say, 'You're no help at all.' Rescuer becomes the Victim. As you can see it becomes interesting and at times confusing to watch the switches. Family games can have players in all positions, and they can change positions quickly.

An adult client recently told me about her mother who insisted (without being asked) on coming over every day (Rescuer) to 'help' her while she was sick (Victim). When mother arrived she then proceeded to criticize (Persecutor): 'Look at the mess in this kitchen, dishes are not done, no food for the kids, now I have to clean up.' My client said her mother has done this to her for years, and my client was feeling inadequate and angry. I invited her to move out of the Victim position and tell her mother she was angry and to stop coming over to help. It is possible that her mother is addicted to being needed and unconsciously sends a message to my client to 'be sick so I can take care of you'. The power of this type of projection can be what causes people to remain sick or in Victim positions. If my client assertively tells her mother to stop coming every day to help, tells her that she is well and will do it herself, she may well get well.

Why do we keep playing games and ending up in bad feelings? You may well ask why we do something that is not fun and is negative.

There are many reasons. Several reasons have been written about in TA literature. The main reason is that by playing a game we are re-playing an outdated strategy for survival. It is a way we learned as a child to get our needs met, and we think as an adult it will still work. Sometimes it does, albeit with negative consequences.

People play games to further their scripts. What does that mean? It means that every time a person plays a game and sets up a repetitive pattern that ends in the same thing happening over and over, and she says, 'see, there it is again, I am stupid' She has reinforced her old script belief, and life position, of I'm not OK, others are OK and life is hard and difficult. Beliefs once again get reinforced. This makes life safe and predictable. We seem to have a fear of stepping into the newness of each day, of stepping into the mystery of life. We want to maintain the drama we know and are addicted to. E. Tolle, (2005. p.77) says our ego (old beliefs) is at war and wants to survive at all costs. He asks the question, 'Can you feel there is something in you that would rather be right than at peace?' 'There is nothing that strengthens the ego more than being right,' (p. 67).

Another reason for games is that they are played to maintain the symbiotic relationships that I discussed above. A person in Parent & Adult will likely play Persecutor or Rescuer games in order to keep the other in Child. The person in Child will play poor me and helpless games to maintain their position- once again a drama to maintain egoic positions.

Games are a way of collecting what Berne called in Transactional Analysis language, 'stamps'. If you are on life's off ramp now (as old as I am) you will probably remember in Berne's day the stamps that were collected from shopping? They are like fly-buy points now. When you collect enough you can cash them in for a prize. Psychological stamps or fly-bys are much the same. Think about times in your life when you might have said, 'If he does that one more time, I will...' Or 'The next time she does not do...I will...'

Then you set a game up for him or her to do the thing so that you can cash in the points and do what your threat was. Points are often cashed in for a guilt-free getting drunk or drugged, guilt free shopping sprees, (I used to love those) or free-from-guilt separations, affairs or divorces: not a positive move of course. It is a game of Ego.

Games are also a way of avoiding intimacy. When people are scared of being close and intimate, they will set up games to create distance to keep others away. Games are also a way of chalking up negative strokes if a person is not acquiring positive ones. Negative strokes are better than none at all.

> *Fear, greed, and the desire for power are the*
> *psychological motivating forces not only between*
> *warfare and violence between nations, tribes,*
> *religions, and ideologies, but also the cause*
> *of incessant conflict in personal relationships'.*
> *Tolle, 2005, p. 12*

E. Tolle talks about 'The Pain Body' (p. 129). He discusses brilliantly how our mind and body are connected, how what we think creates emotion in our body. When we are identified with our minds, lost in our thoughts which are often concerned with past or future, rather than awareness in the Now of life, our bodies react to that, and medical science is now discovering how that affects us in sometimes unhealthy ways. When we hold onto old beliefs and negative feelings, when we become obsessed with a victim position of 'me and my story' (Tolle) we lose connection with now consciousness. 'The voice in the head tells a story that the body believes in and reacts to' (Tolle, p. 135).

The old beliefs from childhood that I have been talking about in this book, Tolle also talks about, showing how people hold onto these beliefs and allow them to impact on their life in the present. Beliefs such as, 'I can't trust people, something is wrong with me, no one will ever love me, money is always scarce, life is a struggle, relationships never work out, I don't deserve love', and so on. These beliefs will continue to be manifested in life when they are held onto. As Tolle says, 'let go of the story, and return to the only place of power: the present Mument' (p, 139).

We need to learn from our past, our past experiences have given us lessons and shaped us into who we have become; much of that is a gift, but let them be memories, let them go, and don't hold onto the stories and beliefs in the present. Old held feelings and emotions need to be dealt with, expressed, and let go. Psycho-therapy is helpful in this process, as well as Emotional Freedom Technique, by Gary Craig (EFT), or Thought Field Therapy by Callaghan (TFT) or one of the other 'tapping' techniques.

If the 'pain body' is held onto, the voice in your head will continue to tell you sad, anxious and angry stories about yourself, others and life. The voice will be blaming, accusing, complaining, and you will be identified with that voice, your ego. Now is then lost (Tolle, p. 147). The addiction to anger, sadness, and fear that I talked about earlier will have set in. Tolle also points this out clearly. When that happens, games will be played to gain a 'fix' to the addiction. Some game drama will be created to produce anger, sadness, or fear.

How do I stop playing games? First step is awareness. Becoming aware that you are playing a game begins to stop the process. As Tolle says, when there is war, it is the ego fighting to survive. We need to step into our witnessing presence, and become aware of what we are doing, watch our actions. Then the power of our ego will lose its grip on us. Then a power far greater than ego will enter our life.

> *The ultimate purpose of human existence, which is to say your purpose, is to bring that power into this world... Only presence can free you of the ego (Tolle, p. 78).*

Using your awareness, there are four options to stop playing your part in a game:

> *Ignore the game.*
> *Play the game, however do so in awareness.*
> *Play another game, (in awareness).*
> *Confront the game.*
> *TA Today, 1987.*

I find the best two options are to ignore or confront. To ignore means that you stop playing your part, be aware it is your ego attempting to strengthen itself, don't get hooked in to your usual response, do something different, don't allow yourself to get into old negative feelings. Perhaps, turn away and go for a walk. Put simply, don't respond to the bait. You could even suggest something such as, 'Let's not play this old game, let's do something fun instead.'

Confronting the game means to speak up and say something such as, 'Here we go again, I'm not doing this, this is not fun and will not create happiness. Can we talk about this and work out how we can stop this old pattern?'

A word of warning! Games usually get worse before they get better. When one person stops their part in games, the other person may well play harder to get the other person back in the old familiar box. Stick to change, and you can eventually break up patterns.

J. James, another TA trainer, constructed a game plan for breaking game patterns. He advises to write the moves in a game by looking at it from the beginning. What happens first? Who says or does what? What happens next, and so on until you have written all the steps of who said and did what. There may well be several steps to the game. At the end, look at what feeling each person experiences. By this time you may have uncovered what is a familiar pattern and familiar feelings. These often end with a return to the same old beliefs about self, others and life.

To break the pattern, look at the process and ask yourself, what is the earliest point that I/we can do something different? Then do that the next time it starts. This may be to not respond in the usual way, or not respond at all, but rather say, 'This is an old game and I'm not going to do this anymore.' If you find that you have gotten caught into games, then at least don't wallow in old feelings and belief systems. Go do something fun.

❦❦❦❦❦

Chapter Nine
Communication, Communication

I have saved the most important issue for last. Communication is most often listed as the number one problem with relationships. We all seem to have problems with talking and speaking our truth. I believe this stems from our early scripting and early experiences. When children hear messages like, 'don't talk back, do as I say, children should be seen and not heard, don't show feelings, don't be angry, stop crying or I'll give you something to cry about,' as a result they learn to be frightened to speak. Clients often have told me in therapy that as children they were frightened to tell Mum or Dad they were angry. Their response is often, 'I didn't dare to, I would have gotten belted, or criticized.'

Children who are shamed at school for having the wrong answer learn to shut up and not take risks. Children learn which things they can say, and which they cannot, and what feelings are OK, and what feelings are not. As adults these people still feel unsafe to speak or feel. Some think the only way to speak is in anger, and using criticisms as Mum or Dad did. When these adults form relationships it is easy to see why communication can be a problem.

I would like to look at communication first from the perspective of Transactional Analysis, (*TA Today*, Stewart & Joines). This literally means to analyze communication. This is done effectively using Ego states model. If I say to you, 'Hello, how are you?' and you reply, 'Fine thanks, how are you?' we have completed a transaction. There are three main types of transactions, Complementary, Crossed, and Ulterior. Transactions involve all the ego states, Parent, Adult and Child.

Positive complementary transactions are the most effective to use the majority of the time. They lead to communication that feels comfortable, 'on the same wavelength,' so to speak, and thus people involved feel like continuing conversations. In this type, one person directs their opening transaction (stimulus) from one of their ego states to one of the other person's ego states, and the other person responds from that ego state as expected.

Here are some examples:

Adult to Adult works well: 'What are your plans for the day?' 'I'm having lunch with friends.' This feels fine, and they may well continue the conversation.

Another example is a conversation between Parent and Child ego states. Parent ego state says, 'You look tired, do you want a back rub? Child ego says, 'Yes, please, I would love that.'

Or two Child egos could be, 'Can we go to the movies today? and the other says, 'Great, that would be fun.'

These examples are positive, but there is another possibility of Parent to Child that often happens, and is not positive. When one person from Critical Parent talks down to the other person's Child, and the other person accepts the Child put down position.
Person A, 'You are so stupid, I don't know why you do...'
Person B, says feeling shamed, 'I'm sorry, I'm such as idiot.'

This type of communicating will maintain symbiotic relationships.
Alternatively, person B could say firmly, 'Don't talk to me like that, I'm not stupid!'

The negative type is something I often see in abusive relationships, and may have been occurring for many years. If a person has a negative belief system. e.g., I am stupid, others are better, they will likely accept criticisms and put downs. If the other believes, I'm better than others, or women are stupid, or I have to be in control to keep it all together, they will inflict the put downs and be abusive.

Crossed transactions are what cause communication to breakdown. When one person sends a transaction to an ego state in the other person, and expects a response from that ego state, but instead receives a response from an unexpected ego state, it causes an uncomfortable feeling. This usually feels hurtful, or anger producing, and the communication breaks down at least temporarily.

Example:

Person A asks 'What are your plans for the day?'
Person B says, with arrogant body posture, 'It's none of your business.'

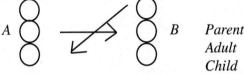

Person A feels hurt, angry and dismissed, does not feel like com municating further. Person B may feel triumphant.

Another example, person A says, 'You look tired, can I help you with something?' Person B says, from Rebellious Child, 'I'm fine, leave me alone.'

Sadly, this type of transaction is often used between parents and children, between partners, and between workplace relationships. If you want to improve communication, keep it complimentary. Talk to your partner, children, friends and family, Adult to Adult as much as possible, not Parent to Child.

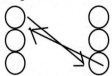

There are of course times when parents need to be firm and set rules; however, it does not need to be done in a critical way. It can be said from an Adult ego state. Most of the time if a person sends a critical message to another, there will be either a communication breakdown, or the other person is going to return a criticism, which usually starts a fight or conflict. Another possibility is a receiver of a critical message will respond from rebellion in some way.

For those of you who are parents, you will no doubt have experienced this. When you say to a child in a angry tone, 'Your room is a mess, get in there and clean it up' the response is something like, 'I'll do it later, I like it that way, your room is a mess too.' Or, they may stomp off to do it, but not do it well.

Ulterior transactions are when two messages are conveyed at the same time. Think about the type of experience you have had when a person has said something to you and on the surface it seems OK, but you feel there is something else going on underneath. There is a felt covert message. The words on the surface may sound and in fact be Adult to Adult, but you feel a hidden agenda.

Example: 'What are you going to do today?' Adult to Adult, on the surface, but when said in a sarcastic, accusing and critical tone, the underlying message may be, 'You are probably going to be lazy today, as usual.' Transactions with a hidden agenda, a covert message, are usually the first step to a game.

The well know ulterior transaction is a person saying to a date, 'Do you want to come in for coffee?' Ulterior meaning, are you interested in having sex?

The rule for this transaction is: *the response given, will be taken by the other as a response to the hidden agenda. A 'Yes' to a coffee invitation will be heard as a yes to sex.*

As we all know communication is much more than just words. Voice tones, gesture, looks, postures, and expressions all play a larger part. Knowing how to cross a negative transaction can be very useful at times. If a person is sending a critical message to you, rather than a returning critical response back, which usually starts a fight, respond from Adult.

Example: Person A says critically, 'You have made a mess with this report.' Rather than being defensive or angry, respond from calm Adult and ask, 'What exactly do you think needs changing?' This will invite them into Adult to answer you. If you want a person to move to their Adult ego state, ask, how, what, when where questions.

Or as I said above, rather than accept a criticism, a put down. or discount, say from your Adult, 'Don't speak to me like that, I don't like it.'

Chapter Ten
Common Communication
Mistakes.

There are two main communication errors that probably all of us have been guilty of at some point in our lives. One is not listening, the other is not respecting the other person's point of view.

Looking first at the issue of different points of view, I am fairly certain that all of you have experienced being in a discussion with your partner at some point where you both have had a different view about something. You see it one way, and he/she sees it another way. What happens then? You usually start arguing about who is right, and who is wrong. It goes something like this?

> *A says, I think what we need to do is...*
> *B says, No, what we need to do is...*
> *A says, That is a crazy idea! That won't work!*
> *B says, How dare you call me crazy!*
> *You are being stupid!*

The uproar fight starts, and the argument escalates. Does this sound familiar? We have all done it.

The first point I make with couples is to discuss this

common occurrence and ask them if they are willing to accept the philosophical position that they are both right. Most often both points of view are right, it is just that both are looking at things from a different angle. And, isn't that interesting! We would be bored silly if we were really all the same. Reality is that we are all one, and each person brings a piece of the whole. When two or more people bring something different to the table, and all parts are included and thought about, the result is the combination is usually better than if only one idea is used. This is synergistic, the sum of the whole is more than the two parts.

Recall the old tale of the blind group who are asked to describe an elephant. Each person went up to an elephant and felt a different part. One person felt the tail, one person felt the ear, one person felt the side, one person felt the foot. Each person then of course had a very different description of what an elephant is like, and all descriptions were in part correct. They needed all points of view to get a whole picture of the elephant. This attitude needs to be adopted in relationships.

Rather than saying, 'You are wrong, how can you possibly see it that way,' instead say, 'That's an interesting idea, tell me how you see it that way.' Listening is a growth process.

> *It [listening] is the process of transiently suspending your own consciousness and allowing the reality of another person's mind to enter yours without evaluation. This stretching of your mind to include the subjectivity of another opens you to new information that is essential for your growth,*
> *Hendrix, 1992, #p.283.*

A model I use with couples is to put both points of view, or both wants and needs on the whiteboard, then get to work on how both people can get what they want. I believe with creative thinking, respectful listening by both, and positive intent, a win/win solution can be found.

Looking at an example about plans for a holiday:

A wants to go fishing, and B wants to stay in a luxury five star hotel. Sounds very different. The first question I ask is, what is it you both want from your plan? A wants to catch some fish and relax somewhere quiet. B wants to relax, and have comfort and fun, not hard work camping. So their wants have some similar components. I then ask them to brain storm how they can both get what they want, and list those ideas. List all the ideas, real possible ones as well as funny crazy ones.

Possibilities:

1. Find a hotel that is close to the sea or a lake for fishing.
2. Go fishing and camping one week and then to a Hotel the other week.
3. Go on separate holidays (not a good option for closeness).
4. Find something different that they would both like.
5. Each go one week to their separate place and then the other week someplace together. They will be happy they have gotten their need met, and be happy to see each other.

You get the idea! All needs and wants can be met as long as you listen, and have the good will to meet the other person's need as well as your own. That is love. It's about listening, giving and receiving. Have you ever heard your partner say to you, 'You are not listening to me? Listening, and letting the other person know you are listening, is a skill. Have you ever been guilty of listening to only the first sentence or two of what your partner is saying to you, and then shutting off listening while you think and plan what your response or argument is going to be in return, as soon as you can get a space to put it in? Then as soon as he/she takes a breath, you jump in with 'But... , or, That's not right, what you need to do is...' This is not listening! Sometimes, you might be listening, but you don't let your partner know you are listening.

Listening is holding your thoughts and ideas until the other person is finished with what they want to say, *and*, mirroring that back to them to let them know you have heard what they said, *before* you say your piece. Example, 'What I heard you say is...,Have I got it right?'

Giving and receiving are important aspects of relationships. If one person is in a position that voices an attitude of 'I want what I want, and that is what I am going to have', then there is no giving to the other. The partner may well feel unimportant and resentful. On the other side if one person takes the position of, 'We'll do what you want, I don't mind', then that person does not receive and ends up feeling resentful and hurt. Both positions harm the relationship. Giving, by having the intent to meet your loved person's needs, *and* receiving your needs by assertively asking are essential. A person who has a Please Me driver frequently has difficulty asking for what they want. They are focused on pleasing. Keep in mind that receiving is a gift you bestow on your partner. We all feel helpful and gratified when we are able to give to our loved person.

The Imago Relationship therapy model gives an excellent process for good communication (Hendrix, 1992). There are three steps to good communication, and they are called the couples dialogue process. The three steps are:

Mirroring
Validation
Empathy

Using this process firstly creates safety. If you stick to the rules you cannot end in a fight or argument. It makes people listen respectfully. I see it as crossing the bridge. When my partner expresses his idea or point of view, I need to suspend all my ideas, cross the bridge to his world, and ask him to tell me about his ideas, and how he sees it his way. Then I mirror that, to let him know I have heard and respected his view. Then, I can ask him to cross the bridge to my world, and I will tell him about my thinking. He will mirror what I have said. This brings respect, and we usually find a way to meet the needs and wants for us both.

Another point about relationships is that one person is a maximizer and the other is a minimizer. Meaning one person talks more, the other is quieter. Think about your relationship: which one of you is the one who 'wants to talk about it', and which one wants to take time out, be alone, go in a cave, or sulk? The talker is the maximizer, the cave person is the minimizer. Either position is fine, there is not a right or wrong one, that's just how relationships are. The dialogue process evens it out. It makes the maximizer slow down, and makes the minimizer talk more. The process is that you will take turns talking and listening. One person will start with talking, and keep it to two sentences (short ones, for the maximizer) at a time. (Don't worry, you will get to say all you want to say, it just needs to be in chunks so the other can get it all and mirror it back to you). The first rule to start is that you need to ask for time to talk, rather than launching straight in with your frustration. Give the other person time to get their head ready to listen, and to make time to give you their full attention. Ask, 'Can I talk to you about something now? If not now when can we do it?'

When one person says,'I would like to talk', then you both need to find a time as soon as possible to sit down and give each other your full attention. Immediately is preferable if possible, and if not, then as soon as possible. The time needs to be created so that there will be no interruptions from kids, work, or other distractions. Don't try to talk while you are doing other things. People don't feel listened to if they are only receiving half your attention.

OK, now you are siting down in two chairs, face to face, heart to heart and close together, and you have created space to not be interrupted.

Person A starts with saying what he/she wants to talk about. State the issue. e.g. 'The issue is.....' Person B mirrors this by saying, 'The issue you want to talk about is...tell me about this.' Mirroring reassures the other person that you have heard the factual content of what they said.

Let us go through an example step by step.

A says, 'I feel angry when you are late, and you don't call to let me know.'

B mirrors this by saying, 'What you are saying is that you feel angry when I am running late and I don't call. Have I got it right? Tell me more about that.'

A then says more. 'When you are late and I have not heard from you, I feel scared that something has happened to you. I get really upset.'

B mirrors again, saying 'When I am late and I don't ring, you feel scared and get upset.' B again asks, 'Is there more you need to say?'

When A has said all she wants to say, and B has mirrored that back, then B validates by saying, 'I have heard what you have said and you make sense.' (This does not necessarily mean that B agrees, but that A's feelings make sense and that B has heard her point of view).

Then B needs to give empathy by saying, 'I can see that you get scared and upset, and then probably angry?'

A can then verify that she feels angry as well as scared if that is true.

Then B takes his turn and responds to what A has said.

'When I am running late, I am usually busy and have lots on my mind and I forget to call you.'

A then mirrors 'What you are saying is that when you are running late, you are busy, and have lots on your mind, Is there more?'

B 'I guess I'm not used to someone caring about me or worrying about me, that did not happen when I was young.'

A mirrors 'You are saying that you are not used to anyone caring about you, that you did not experience that when you were young.'

A can then validate by saying, ' I have heard what you have said and you make sense.'

A empathizes by saying, 'I imagine you must feel hurt about no one caring about you when you were little?'

A, may then say ' Well I do care, and worry, and I would like us to find a way for you to learn to ring me when you are going to be late.'

They can continue this dialogue to finish with this topic, and to find a solution.

When both people have been heard, and respected, the person who feels frustrated can ask for three things that would help solve the problem.

A might say she wants B to be more considerate. That is an OK request, but it's also abstract, B may not really know what he needs to do behaviourally. What does respect mean for her? The requests need to fit the SMART model which is:

> **S**pecific
> *Measurable*
> *Achievable*
> *Relevant to the situation*
> *Time Limited*

A might request something like:

> 1. For the next month, when you are on your way
> home I want you to ring me.
> 2. For the next month if you are not home by 6pm,
> ring me.
> 3. For the next month, every other day, ring me just
> to say hello and tell me you love me.

B is then required to pick at least one of these requests to do for A and give it as a gift. (Never an 'I'll do this for you if you do that for me attitude.)
B may decide to do all three.

Neurologically what usually results is after a person has practised a new behaviour for about a month, a new neuro network has been developed, and people have by then developed the habit of doing it, they will usually continue. The giving person usually finds they like the new behaviour or the results, such as a happier relationship, and enjoy the good feelings they experience from giving. n.p.Note to the receiver of the new behaviour, be sure to voice your appreciation for what your partner is doing for you. That invites more of the same. Remember what I said much earlier about strokes: what you stroke is what you get.

Consider the below outcome with the above situation. It could have gone something like this if they had not used the dialogue process:

As soon as B comes in the door, with an angry critical tone, A says: 'You are an hour late AGAIN, and you did not call. You are inconsiderate, and don't give a damn about anyone but yourself. You are a selfish b......'.

B...'What the hell do you mean calling me selfish, Why do you think I've been out working all day? Who do you think I do this for? Do you think I would do it if it was not for you and the kids, Do you think I like this work? You never appreciate what I do for you and the kids.'

A 'Oh, so it sounds like me and the kids are a bother and a burden are we? Well don't bother.'

B... 'Fine I won't, I'm sick of coming home and getting blasted as soon as I walk in the door.'

I'm sure you can see how this game can easily escalate into third degree, to end up in the divorce court, or with violence. Even if it only goes to second degree, it will end up in anger and bad feeling for perhaps hours or days.

The dialogue process works much better, and usually resolves problems simply by taking the time to really listen, hear and understand your partner. If there are changes to be made, then ask for three requests. One person can ask, 'What I need from you is..., or the other can say, 'What can I do to help you with this problem?'

There is something rather magical that happens when you use the dialogue process on a regular basis. I suggest two to three times per week couples need to set aside time to talk, and to do so by using the dialogue process. It is not something that is only to be used when there are disagreements or conflicts. It is most importantly to be used to maintain connection with each other, and to ensure that you are communicating well. It is too easy to lose connection if we don't work at it. To obtain connection is what we all crave, consciously or unconsciously, and why we form relationships.

Additionally, magic happens in that conflicts and disagreements mostly disappear when couples are connected and dialogue occurs on a regular basis. When two people sit heart to heart and eye to eye, there is a deep sense of connection and a sense of getting our innermost needs met. Often the need to be heard, understood, made to feel important, cherished, and loved was not met in childhood, so that need gets transferred onto your adult relationship. We all have the need to feel connected to a loved person, we are not being 'too needy'. You may not even be conscious that you are longing for these things, or perhaps you learned to 'Be Strong' and shut down your needs. Many conflicts in relationships are about feeling you are not getting your needs met, that something is missing, and you don't know what it is, but it feels empty. So what do you do?

When our needs are not being met we all do the same: we revert to our reptilian brain and do what we did as a baby. We cry, scream, have a temper tantrum, fight, sulk or demand, in an attempt to get our partner to give us what we want. Does this work? No! It creates fights and disharmony. We unconsciously think, If I am not getting positive attention from you, then I will make you give me attention by being angry or sad. However, when both partners sit face to face and heart to heart, and dialogue, intending to listen to each other, and mirror it back so they know we are listening, then this process meets the inner Childs longing to be heard and loved, and most conflicts usually disappear. When we feel this deep connection with our partner, and we know we are being listened to, it gives us that wonderful feeling that we are important, that we are understood, that we are loved, and we feel satisfied and content. There is no need to fight about anything to gain attention.

This is an interesting neurological truth. We all know that for a baby to develop healthily, for its neuro networks to connect for optimal development, the baby needs to enjoy, from the day of birth, loving mirroring from its mother and father. The baby needs to be seen, with a loving gaze, from the eyes of Mum and Dad. When babies are seen, fed, and held, they stop crying. This human need never ends, nor should it. All children need attention, and 'the look of love' from parents, to develop into healthy adults. As adults, we all still need to see the looks of love from important people in our lives, especially our partners. Receiving looks of love, eye to eye, and soul to soul, containing the full awareness of our partner, meets our greatest need. This is where the spiritual quality to a relationship resides. We can literally heal our partner's past wounds, meet their most fundamental need, and regain our own wholeness by giving this gift or love, of loving mirroring.

Many times, couples who have been dialoguing in my office and at home for a few weeks, say something like, 'We have stopped fighting, I can't even remember what we used to fight about, it's just gone, we feel like we are back on our honeymoon, it's wonderful.' In order to bring this transformation about, you need to commit to talking, have a dialogue regularly and certainly whenever you know there is something going on between you that needs talking about. Stay in there, and talk, don't leave or avoid things.

Very sadly what I have often found over my years of working with people is when people as children have not had enough loving connection with parents, caregivers, or siblings, their longing for connection has left an empty hole feeling inside them. In an effort to fill their hole they have become addicted to sex, food, alcohol, drugs, work or some other form of appeasement. Those things only temporarily fill the gap. Soon the longing returns. Real human connection is what is required.

The Imago theory (Hendrix) talks about closing the exits or the invisible divorces. What does that mean? It means *not* using any of the various forms of exits. You know, the things we do to avoid talking. Getting on the computer, going to the shed, going out with friends, getting busy with work, kids, cooking, cleaning, going shopping, and so on and so on. There are many ways a person can avoid being available for talking. I invite you to make a commitment with your partner that when they is some tension between you, that you will stay or return to talk it through. In short, stop running away.

Consider now the instructions for couples dialogue. Use them regularly and watch the magic happen.

COUPLES DIALOGUE

SENDER: The one who wants to send a message must take the initiative and say: 'I would like to have a Dialogue. Is now okay?' These are some main reasons why one might want to have a Dialogue:

       1. You are upset about something and want to discuss it.

       2. You want to discuss a topic that you think might be 'touchy'.

       3. You want to be heard about something important to you.

       4. You want to understand your partner's viewpoint.

       5. You want to spend some quality time with your partner and feel connected.

RECEIVER: It is the receiver's job to grant a Dialogue time ASAP, now if possible. If not now, set an appointment time so that the sender knows when he/she will be heard.

The receiver does three things:

1. **Mirror:**

'What you are saying is ... or Let me see if I got it.'
When there is a natural pause, the receiver will say two things:
a. 'Am I getting what you said?'
b. 'Is there anything more you would like to say about that?'
When the sender has finished sending, the receiver moves on to:

2. **Validation:**

a. The first thing to do is to summarize in a few sentences what has been said:
'In summary what you're saying is ...'
Then check out the accuracy by saying, 'Is that a good summary?'
b. Then say a few sentences like: 'I am listening to you carefully. I follow what you are saying and you make sense.'
Always end up saying the sentence: 'You make sense.' (This

does not mean you agree, just that you understand their point of view).

3. **Empathy:**

'I imagine you might be feeling ...'
Or ' I imagine you might have felt ...'

Then you make some guesses at what the sender is feeling. Feelings are stated in one word (i.e. angry, confused, sad, upset, etc.) If what you guess entails more than one word it is probably a thought ('You feel that you don't want to go with me.' This is a thought, not a feeling). Also, one never knows for sure what another person is feeling. Therefore check out your guess by saying: Is that what you are feeling?'
n.p. When the sender shares with you other feelings, mirror back what you heard. Then enquire, 'Are there any other feelings you are having?'
n.p. Then again mirror what is said.

When the receiver has gone through all three parts (mirror, validation and empathy) then he/she says: 'I would like to respond now'.

Then switch and the receiver now becomes the sender. The process is repeated with the other person talking (Hendrix, 1992).

When the couples dialogue still results in unresolved problems, the person with the frustration needs to ask for three requests that would help solve the problem. Inject requests into the SMART model that I discussed above. When the other person grants at least one wish, and starts to do the requested behaviour, there are as a result growth gifts for both. The receiver of the gift receives healing for their childhood wounds. The giver of the gift will usually find it difficult to do the new behaviour because it calls on them to use parts of themselves they had put away in order to be safe when growing up. However, they will grow and recover their lost functions.

Going back to the above couple, she asked him to call her on his way home from work, and call when he was going to be late. The issue for him was that, as a result of his childhood scripting, he had shut down his thinking and doing capacity to some extent to get along in his family and survive. In order to meet her needs and remember to call, it would require him to use his thinking and do-ing. Doing so activated his capacities back to life, and he became whole again.

When a person is willing to stretch and use lost-self parts of themselves in order to heal wounds in their partner, they will also gain healing themselves and be brought back to wholeness, re-gaining all their capacities. This is, as I mentioned above, the spiritual quality of relationships, and this is what real love is.

Imago therapy has workshops that happen all over the world as well as Imago therapists. **http://gettingtheloveyouwant.com/**

Chapter Eleven
Putting All This Together

To put all this together, by going back to some of the people you met in earlier chapters you will see how all this played out in their lives.

Ann, as you will remember, had a Be Perfect driver, as a result of her critical parents not being satisfied with her school work unless it was perfect. She decided that the only way for her to be good enough was to work hard and strive for perfection. Thus she became an obsessive compulsive personality type, or in a more positive description, a responsible workaholic.

I need to clearly point out that all of us are certain personality *types* and this does not necessarily mean disorder. Most people are in the normal range (or normally neurotic range). We have all decided on behaviour we thought we needed to adopt in order to get along in life, and these become personality types. It is only in the extreme end of the scale that they become disorders.

Ann became an overly thinking and doing person, and she, for the most part, shut off her feelings and sensing. She paid little attention to her own signals of tiredness or stress, and kept working long hours. She also did not allow herself much Child fun time. She became, as you can imagine, very successful in her career from her hard work, but she burnt out as a result.

Ann married David, a rather shy sensitive type, who had a

Please Me driver that he assumed as a result of trying to keep his father happy so that he would feel safe. Ann was attracted to David because of this. He was open to his feelings and sensing, (the denied parts of Ann). David had shut off his thinking and doing because he was often criticized for those as a child by his father. He decided he was not good at doing things since his father would often say, 'You are useless.' David was attracted to Ann's abilities to think and do. They both, at first, felt they had found their other half, and felt complete with each other.

Ann worked hard at her profession, and David went from job to job, not ever really being successful because he did not think or do well at work. They had two children, and Ann went back to work soon after each birth. She worked long hours and when she came home, she did most of the work at home and with the children as well, because David did very little. David focused on trying to please Ann and the children, but not in a responsible way. He was often out with friends.

Ann soon began to see David as immature and irresponsible, and David saw Ann as being absent and too serious; always working and no fun. David had decided as a child that if he stayed childlike he would be taken care of. His mother did everything for him, and he expected that from Ann, believing that was the role of women. Ann, on the other hand decided that she needed to grow up fast and take care of herself. At an unconscious level they fited together well. David wanted Ann to take care of him, and Ann was used to taking care of all that needed to be done, perfectly.

David was often sad, and feared Ann did not love him. Ann was often anxious about not getting everything done right, and depressed about all she had to do. Ann's Child ego state was screaming out inside her, 'What about me?' Ann was not listening to her inner Child, and kept working too hard. They played destructive games in their relationship. Persecutor games by Ann to prove how useless David was. She would set him up to forget something, or do something wrong, and then come down heavy with criticisms and blame. Perhaps she thought that by doing this David would decide to try his best to be perfect, as she had, when she was criticized by her parents. She expected her children to be perfect as well. David played victim games of Poor Me, and Ain't it Awful, hoping to gain Ann's sympathy and get her to take care of him. They had many fights that ended in withdrawal and silence. When they came to therapy they were at a crisis point of possible separation.

Ann wanted David to help more at home, and with their children, and wanted him to grow up. She often felt like he was another child she had to take care of, and she was exasperated at this. Ann wanted an equal partner, not another child. David wanted Ann to stop working so much, and have some fun time with him and the children. He wanted some understanding and expression of her feelings, which is what he did not get from his father. Ann needed his help, and to be loved for herself, which is what she did not receive from her parents.

In addition to these issues, Ann disclosed after a couple of sessions that she had 'met someone' at work, and was attracted to him. She found him interesting and exciting. He was, Ann described, everything David was not. Professional, responsible, intelligent, and hard working. Ann said they had stimulating conversations, and she felt he was on an equal level to her. Their friendship had become sexual, and Ann said she at first felt guilty, but not now since David was 'such a child.' David was devastated, and very hurt when she told him about this friendship. Ann was not sure she wanted to stay married to David, certainly not if things did not change. David wanted very much to save their marriage saying he loved Ann completely.

After a few more consultations, Ann admitted that she was searching for and exaggerating all David's faults, in order to relieve her guilt at having an affair. Ann was playing the game of, If it Weren't For You, telling herself, 'If it were not for David being such a child, I would not be attracted to this other man. David has made me do this.' Once Ann took responsibility for this game, she was willing to stop seeing this other person, and work on their relationship.

To save their marriage, David needed to stretch and regain the use of his thinking and doing and help Ann, which then allowed her more time for fun with him and their children. Ann needed to regain her feelings and sensing and express her feelings. By understanding David's history, she saw him in a different light, and gave him understanding. Ann now does not work so hard and has fun time. David is helping in the house and being an equal grown up partner. They now have love and romance in their relationship.

I have seen this scenario many times in therapy, and know that roles can change. Sometimes it's males in the work hard role and females in the Child position. In same sex relationships, either partner can take either role.

We will re-visit Betty who came from a family where Father was very cruel and violent, both physically and verbally, to mother and children. Betty was oldest in the family, and when Father came home drunk and became violent, it was terrifying to the children who cowered in the bedroom. They feared for their and their Mum's lives. Betty did her best to take care of her siblings and reassure them that things would be OK, even though she was not sure if that was true. She became hypervigilant, and was constantly on watch to see what mood Dad was in when he came home. She tried her best to keep him happy and pleased. Sometimes it worked, often not. Betty's mother was passive, did not stand up to her husband, accepted the violence, and believed it was her fault as her husband told her. He would often say, 'If only you did ..., or didn't do...then I would not get angry. It's your fault I get angry, Betty's mother would give Betty lots of praise for taking care of everything. 'What would I do without you? she would say.

Betty, as a result grew addicted to being a rescuer. She felt good and important when she was taking care of others. Betty, as you can imagine, was often stressed with all the responsibility she took on and had developed irritable bowel syndrome.

Betty married Bob, an angry man who was much like her father. He too was often violent. Bob also came from a family where his father was violent so he thought that behaviour was normal and the acceptable way to treat a wife and children.

Betty followed her mother's pattern and put up with

violence, and thought, 'If only I can please him enough, he will stop.' She took on the Parent and Adult role, and was responsible for everything in the house and child raising. Her addiction to being a rescuer meant unconsciously she didn't let Bob do much. She preferred to do it all, and did it from the martyr role; playing the game of What Would You do Without Me? Betty believed that if only she could find a way to stop Bob from being angry, she could then go back and stop her father from being angry. This is of course totally irrational, but the Child ego state thinks this is possible.

Bob had a Be Strong driver and kept his feelings inside, and felt he had to keep everything in control. His fear as a child was that if he didn't control himself and do everything right, he would be beaten by Father. This was often true. So, as an adult he still carried that fear. He had to keep everything in control. He attempted to control what Betty did, who she saw, where she went, and control money and the children. Betty for years thought if she did what Bob wanted he would be happy. Bob thought a woman's place was to take care of him and the house. He did little to help, thinking his only role was to provide the money for the family. All of this of course did not work, and his violent episodes increased in frequency. Bob played persecutor games by putting Betty down, abusing her and the children verbally to make himself feel superior. Bob did not feel adequate inside as a result of the way his father treated him, and this was a very uncomfortable feeling. To protect himself from this inadequate feeling he would tell himself, 'At least I am better than Betty'.

Bob saw the world as a hierarchy. He did not feel he was at 'the top', but consoled himself with saying, 'at least I'm not on the bottom like, they are'. Of course he had to put other people on the bottom in order to feel superior. He would discount women, children, other races and cultures, other religions. He convinced himself he was better than these people.

It was not until the oldest son reached teen years that he stood up to Bob one night during a violent episode, and told his father that if he didn't stop hitting Betty he would retaliate and call the police. Bob then stopped his violent behaviour.

Research has shown that often violence stops when a person finally firmly says, no more, or calls the police and places charges. This is one aspect of proving the perpetrator does have control of what they are doing, and when they say, ' lost it, I can't control my anger, I snap,' is not true.

The police were called and Bob was charged. After many counselling sessions this family healed and Betty and Bob are still together. The first thing that needed to happen was for Bob to promise that he would never be violent again. He was willing to do that. It took a long time for Betty to build a sense of trust with Bob. They have resolved many of their other issues. Children who grow up in violent homes also have many issues to deal with.

For more information on the issues of domestic violence see my other book, Preventing Domestic Violence by Promoting Non-Violence, (Gregory, 2005).

Laura and Rob were another interesting couple to work with. You will remember Laura from earlier, her mother tried to kill herself and Laura, when Laura was three. Laura was then raised by an Aunt, who Laura overheard saying that she would take care of Laura, until she grew up. Laura hearing this decided not to grow up and stay childlike in order to be taken care of. She was afraid that if she grew up she would be abandoned. In order to stay childlike, Laura would become helpless, not think, and depend on others to do things for her. She would often get sick with a variety of ailments such as colds, flu, headaches, back problems, shingles and other illnesses over many years.

Rob was the eldest son in his family. His father was a violent, abusive alcoholic, and he left the family when Rob was eight. Rob's mother had a breakdown at that time, and from then was often sick and bedridden. Rob became the 'man of the house' taking care of his mother and siblings. He received lots of recognition and praise for being responsible and taking care of them, and he became addicted to doing everything in order to feel worthwhile and gain praise for it. In his work he was also responsible, and often did more than his share of work and helped his work mates. He was a good employee and valued by his employer. His peers at work sometimes felt irritated with him because he would often work harder than they did, and show himself to be better than them. He would often take over, and do their work for them which made then feel inadequate.

Robs' belief about women was, they were usually sick and helpless creatures that needed to be taken care of. When Laura and Rob met, the unconscious attraction they felt for each other was a perfect match into their script beliefs. Rob saw women as helpless and needing to be taken care of, and Laura wanted to be taken care of, had learned to be sick in order to obtain nurturance. For the early years of their marriage, they continued in this symbiotic role with Rob being the Parent and Adult, and Laura being the Child. However, after some years Rob became tired and angry at having to do everything. Laura was often sick when he got home from work, and he would do the cooking and cleaning of the house. He had little time for fun. He became very irritated with Laura, did not want closeness or intimacy. Part of my analysis was that sex with Laura felt to Rob like he was having sex with a child, and that was abhorrent to him. Rob saw Laura as a helpless child for whom, he did not feel any sexual attraction. He also early in life decided that women did not like sex, (he had heard his mother tell a friend this), and he decided that he would never force himself on a women. He learned to take care of himself through masturbation.

Laura felt rejected and unloved, and thought the way to be loved was to become more helpless. She got sicker, and had to quit her job, she often had her friends drive her places, saying she 'could not cope.' Laura and Rob were stuck in these positions for many years until Laura finally came to therapy. After some months she began to understand the sick helpless Child role she had adopted, and games that both she and Rob were playing to keep the dynamics going. Laura decided to start using her Adult and grow up. The change in her was delightful. Rob has since decided he is worthwhile without having to care for everyone, and he is affording some time for himself for having fun. They still have issues to deal with, but they are getting there.

The games they were playing were: Rob playing Rescuer games of; What Would You Do Without Me, You Need Me, and I'm Only Trying to Help. When he got angry he would switch to Persecutor and play; Now I've Got You, to prove that Laura was hopeless and helpless. Laura would play Victim games of Poor Me and Ain't It Awful. She would often go to her friends and spend hours telling them how bad Rob was, to gain their sympathy. When she got angry, she would switch to Persecutor and play, Now I've Got You, to prove he was an inadequate husband.

Jill, who you met earlier, never felt loved or wanted in her childhood she married Jack, a loving man who loved Jill very much, however, Jill found it hard to accept. She did not believe she was lovable, and often sabotaged situations to prove that Jack did not love her. She found it very hard to be happy and not depressed. She had become addicted to these feelings and beliefs from her childhood. Her defence from childhood was to be angry and fight back. She often got angry and with Jack, and then when he retaliated she would say, 'See, you don't love me', Jill would then feel depressed and sometimes suicidal. Because of Jill's deep belief of not being wanted, and feeling she should not exist, she had problems with smoking and alcohol. She often got drunk. This can be an unconscious way of killing oneself.

Lynn and George married some time after meeting, and the main dynamic in their relationship was Lynn working hard to prove she was useful. She would especially do work with tools, and do jobs that men usually do. Friends would notice and praise her for it. This was her way of proving to herself and others she was OK. However, this led to George feeling useless and inadequate, and he from childhood had decided not to do things he did not want to do, and used his 'bad shoulder' as an excuse. Lynn projected the helpless child role onto George, and he for years became like 'her eldest child.' Finally during therapy, Lynn realized that she was projecting onto George, and that she was not giving him a chance to do things because she did them first. She changed, and their relationship improved. George began to be responsible and share the workload.

I have often found that women complain about their partners being 'like a child.' Often this true, with men taking the Child
position and using passive behaviour of doing nothing. Many men
have grown up with their mothers doing everything for them, and
they expect their partners to carry on in the same role. However,
on the other hand, women need to look at what part they are playing in this. They may well be treating their partners like children
and doing things for them, taking on the mothering role, because
they have a Please Me driver and a need to feel important. Additionally, many of us women, I believe, have been taught to take
care of others, to please others first, to put our needs last, so we
often train our partners to expect this. Thankfully, I now see many
younger women rejecting this traditional scripting.

Relationships need to be based on equality, with both people using their full potential. Often one person feels that if their
partner becomes competent and capable, then he/she will lose
power. In reality, when both people in a relationship use their full
capacities, then the sum is greater than the two parts. The point to
keep in mind is to use your personal power to function out in the
world to become all that you both can be.

Reach your full potential, and do whatever it is that is your
mission or direction in life. It's not wise to use your power against
your partner in relationship struggles. You are a team, and together
you can do great things for and with each other, for your children
and family, and for the world. It is not about being in opposition to
each other. Honour the differences in your partner, and know that
you have been brought together for a purpose. Your differences
are needed to create a balance, and bring a wholeness together.
When we reach the synergistic stage of relationship, part of it is
about creating something together that we could not create alone.
What do each of you bring that is needed to be used in your mission or your partnership?

A simple example of what I mean is the very important
role of parenting. Often one partner is the softer more permissive
one, and the other is the firmer more disciplinarian one. It is not
about who is right and wrong, it is about both roles being right and

needed, to bring balance.

Changing Partners

Often people in unhappy marriages believe if they leave and find a new partner they will be happy: the grass would be greener syndrome that most of us have considered at some point in our lives. 'If only' I had married someone else! Sometimes it works to find a new partner, but often not. Certainly if there are extreme issues such as domestic violence, abuse, alcoholism that are not being dealt with, then leaving may be the best option. However, often changing partners simply means changing problems.

No one is perfect, and there will always be issues to deal with. Leaving a marriage and changing partners is often just changing problems, and it is usually costly and hurtful to many people. Marriage is about growing, learning lessons, and dealing with issues. Working through difficult times is what it is about, and what brings growth. However, having said that, if one partner refuses to make changes, grow, or deal with issues, it makes it difficult. Perhaps leaving is necessary.

Importantly however, keep in mind that it is not impossible for one person to create changes. Systemically, when one person in a system changes, then the whole system will change in some way- not always immediately positive but often in a way that can lead to positive change. Let me give you an example. In the serious situation of domestic violence, if the victim changes from accepting or putting up with violence to becoming firm, and placing charges, and saying clearly, 'I will no longer tolerate your behaviour. If you are violent again I will call the police, and have you changed' often the violence stops at this point. One person becoming assertive and firmly saying she will not tolerate violence will often eventuate the stopping of the violence.

If there are problems with differences in parenting styles, if one parent does research, and learns about good parenting skills, and puts these into action, the other parent may well see the success and make changes.

It is often the case that one person in a relationship changes sooner or faster than the other partner, and I think this is fine. Perhaps the reluctant person has some fears about change. 'Who will I become?' 'What will happen to us?' I think this person often waits and watches the other's changes to see if they are safe. If one person will take the courage to step into changing they can create the necessary changes in their system and show the other person the way.

❧❧❧❧❧

Chapter Twelve
Making changes

You by now, I hope, have understood some of your past issues, and where they came from and how they developed. An old mentor of mine likened scripts to old family videos that we all carry around in our heads. Unfortunately, they aren't always 'funniest home videos'. For many of you, this understanding alone can bring changes. The main decision to make at this point, is to decide that past is past and leave what you don't want in the past. Let it go, and get on with your lives now. Don't let the past rule your future. Holding on to a negative restrictive past serves no positive purpose. The past cannot be changed. Learn from it, and leave it. Keep the good parts, the valuable lessons, what you learned from your childhood experiences; let the rest go, say goodbye to it.

For example, my parents taught me to do many things well, like using tools, cooking, fishing, and being good with money. I will keep those things, and value them. Other things, I have let go.

Next questions are, what do you want to keep and what to let go of or change, and how to make changes? As I said above, simply understanding issues is frequently often enough to change. People say they understand in their heads what the problems are, and what they need to change, and in fact have succeeded in making changes; however, some old feelings are still present. You may do things a better way, conduct relationships in an improved way, but at the same time still feel some of the old anxieties and sad feelings. Why does this happen you may ask? That comes from making changes in your Adult ego state, which can be helpful. However, to achieve deep changes to feelings, changes need to involve your Child ego state. That is where most old feelings are stored. It was your Child that made the initial decision, therefore your Child ego state needs to make the redecision. That is one of the main reasons that Redecision therapy works so well. Redecision works with the Child ego state, and thus changes the feelings, as well as the Adult understanding

If you continue to be stuck with negative feelings then you may choose the option of going to a Redecision therapist to make your desired changes. You can find a redecision therapist by going to http://.www.wpata.com.au, or, http://www.itaa-net.org/ Of course many other therapists are helpful as well.

The complete Redecision process, I feel, needs to be done with your therapist or counsellor for safety. The process of being in your Child ego state while facing your parent can bring up strong feelings, feelings that you may not be aware are still inside, so I want to ensure your safety by asking you to do this deep work with a therapist.

I do believe some lighter personal work can be accomplished on your own. Redecisions can be made on many levels, and using differing memories or events. However, let me say again and most importantly, that if you have or have ever had issues with suicidal feelings, then you need to do your work with a therapist to ensure your safety. A person should firstly decide they have a right to live, and live happily, and that they will live to a ripe old age. Then they can make other decisions about how they will live. If you decide to do any of this lighter work on your own, you may want to have a friend be there with you for support.

This process of making new decisions can be used with all the drivers, injunctions, games and other behaviours you want to change. Do only one at a time. Trying to do too many at one time loses potency, and each one needs a little time to integrate. You can make many changes by writing it through in your journal. You can imagine having a conversation with a parent, and telling them how you will now be different. Another way could be to write them a letter (that you will not send) telling them the changes you are making.

Once again, only work with situations that are not too traumatic, ones you feel comfortable going through. Any that are more hurtful or scary, take to a therapist.

Another powerful way to make new decisions is to work with your dreams. If you have a dream that is disturbing in some way, then imagine going back into the dream, and imagine a new ending. How would you like the dream to end? Create it any way you want. It is your dream, and you can create anything. It does not have to stick to rules of reality. For example, bring in a strong person to help you, imagine someone telling you just what you need to hear to support yourself. A fairy godmother, or a strong protector, an animal, or a religious figure such as Jesus, or Mary. Create circumstances that will make you feel safe. Then write about this in your journal. You can go on a quest to find a talisman symbol of some sort to keep with you to remind you of the changes you have made. Mary Goulding, one of the originators of Redecision therapy, has a wonderful book, *Who's Been Living in Your Head*, that is helpful with this work. You can find many TA books, and other books, on www.kerry's books.

Changing Rackets or Inauthentic Feelings

The most effective way I know for making changes to your habit of getting into inauthentic or manipulative feelings, such as sad, sulking, anger, or confusion, (or others) in order to play a game in some way, is to promise yourself that you will not stay in racket feelings for more than 10 - 20 minutes. As I mentioned before, real feelings (apart from grief) only last 10 - 20 minutes. If you hold onto them for longer, then probably you have turned them into a Racket. When people realize they can only maintain a Racket feeling for 10 minutes, instead of 10 hours, or 10 days, (even 10 months or years) they usually decide that the fun and profit have gone out of the game. They stop playing, and let the feeling go. So...make a contract with yourself, drop all negative feelings after 10 minutes. Watch the feelings when they occur, become the observer, and in 10 minutes you will feel them dissipating. (You can occasionally have a 20 minute wallow if you must.)

Another aspect is to ask yourself what real feeling are you hiding under the Racket feeling. If you were not feeling, for example, anger, what would you be feeling? Often anger covers sadness. You need to ask yourself what you need to do with your sadness. Perhaps you need to tell someone else what it is they are doing that is causing you to feel sad. You can ask them to change something. The same is true if you find that your Racket is sadness that might be covering anger. You may need to express your real feeling of anger, in a safe way, and ask for some change to occur. The main aspect of change is to stop using Rackets to manipulate people or situations and deal with whatever is happening in a clear productive straight way. Acting out with feelings does nothing to solve the problem.

At times people get stuck in Rackets because unconsciously they hold onto a totally irrational belief, a belief that says, If I stay angry or sad (or whatever the feeling is) long enough, then he/she/they/it will change, or, he/she/they will be sorry for what they have done to me. This is not a clear way to bring change. It is best to ask for change clearly, and not resort to game playing and holding onto Racket feelings as a form of punishment. Sometimes people hold onto the Racket feeling thinking they will make parents from the past change, or be sorry. This is totally irrational because, the parents may not even be around, and if they were here to change today, it would still not change the past. The past is past. Let it go.

A wonderful therapist I trained with many years ago often said to us, 'Imagine that your parents came one day, and knocked on your door and said they realized the mistakes they had made, and they were now going to move in with you so they could make up for it.' Would you really want them to move in with you now? I suspect most everyone would say, 'No!'

A simple process to deal with dropping feelings:

1. Ask yourself, What am I feeling?
2. What can I do about it?
(write down all possible options.)
3. Choose which one you will do,
or you may at times choose not to do it.
4. Do it, or don't do it.
5. DROP THE FEELING!

When you know that you have made the decision to do it or not do it, then you know that it is your responsibility to drop feelings.

24-Hour Rule, and Wall of Trivia

I usually invite couples to agree to a 24-hour rule that I have devised. This means when something happens between a couple and bad feelings have resulted, then the person has 24 hours to bring it up and talk about it. If the person does not do it within 24 hours, then it needs to be dropped, and it is never to be brought up later as ammunition. Months or years later, it is not fair to attack your partner with, 'Remember last year when you...'

If there is not a space to talk within 24 hours, at least put it on the agenda, by saying something like, 'This weekend I would like to talk to you about...'

This rule needs to be put in place *after* all past issues that have formed the wall of trivia have been brought out and discussed. Otherwise the wall will remain. I invite you to talk with your partner about all the past issues and resentments. You need to tell your partner about all past hurts, resentments, and frustrations, and do so in a clear non-abusive manner. Doing this will clear the wall of past issues and then you and your partner will be current: then put the 24-hour rule in place.

The 24-hour rule is excellent with all relationships, friends, parents, children, and other family members. It ensures that people with feelings take responsibility for either talking about how they feel, or if they choose not to, then to drop feelings. Choosing not to *at times* is OK, but don't do it too often, or the wall of trivia will form again. Most of the time it is best to talk about it. People are not mind-readers (as much as we wish they were). By not telling people you are upset about something, you are not giving them a chance to change, and improve the relationship. Additionally you are not being honest. There are two forms of lying. One is of com-mission, telling an untruth. The other is a lie of omission; not say-ing when something is wrong, and leading others to believe all is OK when it is not. The classic example, is when a furious and steaming person, says, 'I'm fine,' when asked 'what is wrong?' This is unfair and does not allow the other person to apologize, or change, or even know what the problem is. The extreme is a situ-ation I have seen several times. One person leaves the relationship and the other had no idea that he/she was unhappy, or that there was a problem. They did not see it coming at all. This is unfair as leaving without voicing frustrations does not give the other person a chance to change and repair the relationship.

Self-Reparenting

Self-Reparenting is a process of caring for and loving your inner Child ego state. It is a process of learning to use your Nurturing Parent within yourself to care for you, rather than using your Criti-cal Parent to criticize yourself. Many people have a habit of being self-critical, and some people take it further to self-harming.

I think I would be safe in saying that most people at some time in their lives are self-critical. Saying to yourself things such as, 'You are stupid, you messed that up, how useless are you, you are, bad, ugly, fat', and on and on. This kind of self talk creates low self-esteem, depression, anxiety, and low self-confidence. You need to stop this kind of self-talk. To bring awareness of the need to change this internal dialogue, I often ask people if they would talk to their children, or best friend that way? Of course you would not! So don't talk to yourself this way either.

Begin to use your Nurturing Parent and talk to yourself in a positive way. Say things to yourself such as, 'You are wonderful, lovable, capable, and a beautiful person.' Acknowledge what your skills are, what you are good at: all people have skills. Think of ways you would encourage your child, or your friend, and talk to yourself the same way. Find a picture of yourself as a child, and put this somewhere you will see it everyday: on your mirror, on the fridge; and talk to your picture in a positive way each day. 'Hello beautiful!' 'You are wonderful.' It may feel strange or silly at first, and you may not believe it at first, but do it anyway. Act as if you do believe it. Old habitual neuro networks take time to change. Eventually as you build new networks, you will start to believe what you are saying, and your life and feelings will change. It does not take too long.

Self-harming

Self-harming can be along a continuum from mild self-harm such as not eating well, or not getting enough sleep or exercise, to working too hard and not taking holidays, to the extreme end of physically harming self. Smoking, drinking too much alcohol, using drugs are all forms of self-harming. Living dangerously, such as dangerous driving or doing dangerous sports without using good safety equipment, are other examples. Physical self-harm, such as cutting self, are at the extreme end and very dangerous. People at this end may well need to see a therapist to learn self-care. Again, a question to ask yourself is, Would you give that, or do that to your child? Would you want your child, or best friend to be doing that behaviour? If the answer is no, then stop doing it to yourself, and if you need help to stop, please see a psychotherapist or counsellor. You are worth it! You have a right to live, and live happily, and be healthy.

Journals and Teddy Bears

Two seemingly simple but very powerful ways of working with self are with the use of journalling and using teddy bears. In my opinion, these two processes are helpful to do life-long for all.

Journalling is done by having a writing dialogue between your Parent ego state and your Child ego state. It is having a conversation with a child you want to get to know, and love.

With your dominant hand write something such as, 'What are you feeling today? What do you want to tell me? What are you needing/wanting from me? What do you want to do today? What do you like doing?' The possible topics to converse about are endless. With your non-dominant hand write your answer. The reason for using your non-dominant hand is that it gets you into your Child ego state. Writing with that hand is difficult, and doing so takes you back to being a child. So stay with that hand when conversing from your Child, even though it is slow and tedious. It is very powerful, and I have experienced for myself and with clients that it can bring enormous changes and awareness. Do this at least 2 -3 times per week, life-long, for optimum emotional health and happiness. Your Child ego has the same needs as you did when you were a child: the needs to be listened to, paid attention too, have needs met, and be loved, and have fun with are life-long.

Ask your Child ego state, what he/she needs from you? Notice how you feel hearing this, are you willing to meet the needs? Sometimes a person has decided their inner Child is not OK and that she does not deserve love and care. This may be a mirror from the way a person was treated as a child. If this is your feeling about your Child, change your belief to a positive one. If you need help with that, find a therapist or counsellor to help. All people are OK and deserving of love.

Teddy Bear work is similar to the above. Get yourself a Teddy Bear, or something similar if you don't already have one. A pillow will do. One that will be you as a child. This is private work, between you and your Child ego state, and you probably will not feel comfortable doing this is front of others. The space between you and your Child needs to be kept private and honoured. Spend lots of time holding and talking to your Teddy Bear. I have found in my years of working with people that when a person has not had enough hugs, holding, being cuddled when a baby or child, the person is left with what I call 'a hole in the soul' or the 'flaw system' I spoke about earlier, meaning that the person often has a feeling of emptiness around their heart center, or chakra, and feel a need to fill this emptiness. Many people, as mentioned earlier, attempt to fill this hole in unhealthy ways: excesses such as filling self with food, compulsive sex, drinking and/or drugging, buying material things, all of which are not successful at filling the hole. These only bring temporary relief. What is needed is lots of contact with the heart chakra area. One of the ways I diagnose this hole with clients, is to ask if they often find that they sleep with a pillow held to their heart area, or often hold a pillow, or their hand, on their heart area. Unconsciously, people often know they need more filling or touch in their heart. Using the Teddy Bear held tightly in a hug over the heart will begin to fill this hole. It may take as much as a daily (or more) hug for a year or two.

Give yourself a hug a day with your Teddy Bear, and tell your Child ego self that you love yourself, and that you are OK and lovable. This work in time will increase your self-esteem and confidence, and you will feel more at ease and comfortable with your self. When you know you are lovable and loved by your grown up self, then you will not need to have that confirmed by others so much. Then you will be with other people because you want to be with them, rather than needing them to tell you that you are OK. People who engage compulsively in many sexual partners usually do this not for need of sex, but for the need to feel loved and lovable. Tell yourself you love you, and believe in yourself. I believe it's true that we cannot love others until we love ourselves. Love thyself has been a spiritual message for centuries.

Self-love is *not* selfish and there is no need to feel guilty about self-love and self-care. Sometimes, if you have been around others who like to be rescued, then as you make changes and become more self-caring, they may call you selfish. They may say,

'You are being so selfish now, what has happened to you?' I invite you to respond by saying, 'Thanks for noticing, I have been working on caring for myself, it's good to see I am achieving my goal.' Self-care does not mean you will become selfish, it means you will care for yourself as well as others. When you don't want to do something, you may say 'No, I don't want to do that', Practise saying No; it's fun and empowering. It's far better to say No to a request, rather then saying Yes, and then resenting it. Your resentment will show and may disrupt situations. Better to be straight and say 'No thanks'. (Within reason or course, at times we do have to do things we don't want to do, and when that happens, then do something nice for yourself in return.)

You can also use your Teddy Bear to change components of your script. Sit your bear in a chair in front of you, or hold him/her on your lap and talk to your bear. Say things such as, 'You don't have to please others all the time, you can please yourself, it's OK to have fun time, you don't have to work all the time, it's OK to show your feelings to others, It's OK to ask for what you want. You get the idea I'm sure. Encourage your child self, be your best friend, promise to keep yourself safe and not let anyone hurt you, and promise you will protect yourself. As I said this is a good daily practice for the rest of your life.

Let your child self know that when he/she was a child that you, being the grown up adult, was not there, but now you are there, and you both will always be together every minute of every day, and you will be your best friend. Often clients report that when they do this work they begin to feel very comfortable with themselves, and enjoy spending time alone with themselves in a way they never did before. Having time and fun with your best and closest friend, You, is a wonderful way to spend time. Enjoy you! Enjoy being with yourself! It is not harmful or silly!

❦❦❦❦❦

Chapter Thirteen
Forgiveness

The final and perhaps most important aspect to this section, dealing with the past, is forgiveness: forgiveness of others and forgiveness of self. Holding onto anger, bitterness, fears, victimhood and blame for what someone has done to you in the past does not serve you well. Doing that will keep you stuck. Staying stuck in the past and holding onto those negative feelings and beliefs will lower one's vibration level. This is the same for those who stay stuck in blame and guilt toward one's self.

For every minute you are angry you lose sixty
seconds of happiness,
Ralph W. Emerson

In order to create the life we want, to manifest positiveness in our lives, we have to have a higher vibration level. What do I mean by vibration level? Think of it as an energy field or aura that surrounds us. It is a constant field of vibrating energy responding to our conscious thoughts. Loving, happy, compassionate, grateful, peaceful thoughts vibrate at a much higher level than angry, bitter, blaming, sad, or guilt thoughts. We have all at some time in our lives experienced being in the company of another person who is emitting negative vibes caused by anger or bitterness. Being in their company drains our own energy, and lowers our vibration, as well as their own.

It is my belief and experience, as it is of many others, that the energy and vibration level of our planet is shifting and rising. We are in the process of awakening. With higher vibrational levels manifestations happen more rapidly. Have you noticed that now when you ask for something it is there much faster than ten years ago? Negative beliefs of 'people mistreat me, life never works for me, or I never get the good things in life,' may well be manifesting the repeat pattern of those events. 'Why does the same thing keep happening to me over and over?' people ask. That is why. The same negative beliefs are being broadcast.

Coming to forgiveness requires accepting that for *some* events, we have played a part in what has shown up in our lives. Not all, I hasten to say. I can hear an angry voice of, 'I did not ask for ...to happen in my life.' Yes, some bad things happen to good people for no apparent reason. However, be willing to consider that for some events there may be some old beliefs lurking in the background.

All events do have some positive outcome to them, as well as the negative. In addition, all experiences have some learning attached. I know this is difficult to see and understand at times. The work of John Demartini (*The Breakthrough Experience* 2002), and Colin Tipping, (*Radical Forgiveness* 1997) discuss these phenomena in depth.

When I say 'no apparent reason', what I mean is that many things happen on a spiritual level that we do not understand. We came into this life to learn lessons and grow; therefore many people, and events in our lives have been brought to us for our growth. I know all that has happened to me in my life has made me who I am. The difficult events and people have made me grow in strength, determination and assertion. I have developed understanding and compassion with clients I see, because to some extent I have been there too. I hope you get the idea. I know it's a difficult one.

I remember being in a workshop with J. Demartini shortly after 9/11. He was being challenged to find positives from that event. As horrible and tragic as it certainly was, the positives were that people came to appreciate the police and firefighters as never before. People of New York came together in compassion and help for each other as never before. So with an open mind, I invite you to think of the positives that you have experienced from even the worst people and events. H. Hendrix, the developer of Imago relationship theory, says we are meant to be in relationship with a person who is the most difficult for us to get along with, because they will bring us growth. We of course are difficult for them, and bring them growth as well. Often people who are the most difficult in our lives are our greatest teachers. Isn't life fascinating and hard to understand at times?

Colin Tipping in *Radical Forgiveness* (1997) believes there is a divine hand present in each Mument, and there is a deeper meaning and purpose in life that we can't always see at present. We are being taken care of at a spiritual level each Mument. I know it does not always feel like that, but the Universe is moving you in directions of healing and growth. We need to get to the place of forgiving others, even thanking them, for being difficult, for the growth and development they have brought us.

In becoming willing to forgive, you let go of control and surrender it to Spirit. He takes care of the other ten percent' (p. 25, 1997). We were given free will in this life to make our own choices, which means we have to willingly choose to be healed and guided by spirit. Tipping says, 'We are not human beings having an occasional spiritual experience; rather we are spiritual beings having a human experience' (p. 40, 1997).

Once again, as Tipping also says, change old negative core beliefs such as, 'They made me like this, If it was not for her I would be OK, I will never succeed, I don't deserve'. Forgive them, even thank them and yourself for your growth, and move on. Let go of the archetypal victimhood many have been addicted to for eons (Tipping, p.73). Being willing to release being a victim will be the key to health and spiritual evolution. Drop self destructive defence patterns such as alcohol and drugs and Ain't It Awful, Poor me games, which are creating illness, dramas, or putting yourself on the bottom of the list. Make today the first day of the rest of your life.

147

❦ ❦ ❦ ❦

Chapter Fourteen
Neuroscience

Now that you have cleared, or are clearing, your past issues, you are ready to move on to creating what you do want from your life. You can now create happiness in your life. You may now have decided what changes you need to make to your beliefs and behaviours. To do this, I now want to present how change occurs in our brains.

New discoveries in neuroscience help us understand how the brain is developed by early experiences. There has been an age old argument: is the development of our character and personality more nature, or is it more nurture? The truth is that it is both. I am not a neuroscientist, so I am going to put this in simple terms as I understand them, and if you want to learn more I suggest you read Louis Cozolino, *The Neuroscience of Psychotherapy,* 2002, or Joe Dispenza, *Evolve Your Brain,* 2007. Other writers to explore are Schore and Siegel. I will be using some of their ideas, and others, to give you my understanding.

I am not going to get lost in talking about the triune brain, reptilian, paleomammalian, cortex, neocortex, and other structures of the brain. Joe Dispenza's book does that well. What is important for me to say here is that the brain does have plasticity: meaning the brain is not hard wired at birth; it continues to develop for a long time after birth, and can be changed and evolved throughout life. This fact has both positive and negative aspects to it. The positive is that with good parenting experience children develop a positive brain structure and function. The negative is that with dysfunctional parenting experiences children may develop in maladaptive ways. Most of these negative issues can however be changed by engaging in therapy.

The nature/nurture argument has been one where some people believe that nature alone determines who we are. They believe that at birth we are hard wired: we are born with our personality, traits, and certain behaviours to a large extent; and it is this nature that defines who we are. The nature belief is that the brain is fully developed at birth and can not be changed. Others, on the other hand, believe it is not about nature, but rather the way children are raised, early experiences and what they decide about those experiences, that shape who they become.

The answer is that it is both. We are born with certain aspects to our personalities, certain traits or possibilities of how we could develop. Think of these as switches that have an on/off button. It is our experiences that turn these switches on, or off. The brain in fact grows and continues to develop long after birth. We are born with certain genetic hard wiring such as instinctual behaviour patterns, the instinct to survive. But the brain does have plasticity, and can and does change. New combinations of nerve cells and neurotransmitters can change in response to new input.

Spiritually, this make sense. If we were hard wired at birth with no possibility for change, then what would be the point of life? I believe our life is about learning lessons, using our free will to choose the right paths, to evolve, and strive toward enlightenment. Quantum physics now tells us that there is a field of all possibilities to choose from; and it is our free will that we were given, that allows us to choose a spiritual path or not. We can, as the Dalai Lama says, train our mind for happiness.

One example of the effects of parenting is, how the way we were raised by our early caregivers, usually parents, formed our attachment mode, (Bowlby, 1971). If we experienced a safe and secure attachment with our caregivers, then we learned to be secure and confident. However, if our experience of caregivers was that they were not safe to be around or did not provide security, then that experience may have switched on a feeling of abandonment, or the child may in fact have been abandoned. The result of those experiences may well develop into a fear of abandonment and usually causes problems throughout life if not treated.

A principle of imprinting may exist for humans as well as it does for animals to form attachment patterns. A child's early environment may be imprinted in the brain by shaping the child's neural networks, and establishing the biochemical set points. These structures and processes then serve as infrastructure for later intellectual skills, affect regulation, attachment and the sense of self (Schore, 1994; Siegel, 1999, cited in Cozolino, p. 13).

We know for a baby to develop normally it needs to have attention, mirroring from the eyes of mother and father. The baby needs to experience a look of love from the eyes of its parents, or caregivers. From this love from their eyes, a soul to soul connection is maintained, and healthy synapse connections are made. Children at all ages continue to need attention and a loving look from parents. For a child to feel loved, she needs to see love coming from her parents' eyes.

We never outgrow this need to see the look of love from the other. That is what nourishes a relationship. We long for and enjoy seeing our partner look at us, in our eyes, soul to soul, with an adoring look of love. Loving looks nourishe us. If a child has been deprived of loving connections with parents, problems with self-esteem may well develop. Depression may certainly develop when there is a lack of expression of love for children, and likewise in adult relationships.

Neuroscience has recently shown that psychotherapy can help rebuild the brain and bring change for people. This process of change and cure has a great deal to do with clients having a new experience in the relationship with their therapist. To experience a warm and secure relationship with a therapist can give a person new beliefs about themselves, others, and life. Clients can learn to feel secure, rather than an having an abandonment fear, with a therapist who is fully present. Human brains are constantly stimulated to grow, and change in reaction to positive and negative experiences with others and events. The nature of relationships we have with others affects our brain and mind. This is where nature and nurture become one (Cozolino, p. 16). When early parenting experiences have not been optimal often symptoms arise that require psychotherapy to change and heal.

What does all this mean? To create lasting change we need to create new neuro networks, new neurotransmitters in our brains. Our brains have developed millions of synaptic networks or patterns. These patterns mean that we tend to repeat the same behaviour over and over. These behaviours become habit, if you like. If we do something many times, or have a belief that we hold onto, it creates a pathway similar to a river that has been formed from water flowing the same way over eons. Think of a pile of mud, then think of a stream of water being poured on top of the mud. The water will develop ruts in the mud as it flows downward. As the water continues to be rained on top, the ruts will get deeper and deeper. To form a new way for the water to find its way down, old ruts will need to be closed off, then the water will find a new path.

It is much the same with our brains. To make changes, old patterns or synaptic networks need to be stopped, and new ones formed. Neuroscience has shown that networks that are no longer used die off in time. Therefore to make changes we need to stop acting out old behaviours, or stop thinking in old negative patterns; we must change old beliefs to new ones, and in time these will become new neuro networks, and become ingrained in our thinking. From these changes new chemical reactions can also develop, and thus feelings and emotions can change.

When I work with clients who are wanting to implant new beliefs they often get stuck because when they tell themselves the new messages, such as 'you are lovable and a good person', at first it does not feel real or true. They tell me they say it but don't believe it so they stop. The old adage, 'Fake it until you make it', applies here. At first it will not feel real and you won't believe it until your new neuro networks develop. Keep at it; it will in time start to feel real and you will then have your new positive beliefs entrenched, and your old negative networks will have died off.

To create change it is helpful to experience an enriched environment that stimulates learning and growth, one that offers warmth, compassion, safety, and a positive relationship. This can be achieved in a loving relationship with a partner as Hendrix says, or with a therapist, or in mild cases, with a friend. A negative environment offers little chance of growth and change.

Through experiencing a positive relationship people can in time learn to regulate their own feelings and emotions better than they could before. In a client-therapist relationship, clients are encouraged to feel and express old held and feared emotions, within the safety and psychological holding pattern with their therapist. Thus, clients learn that those emotions can be expressed safely, regulated, and held by themselves. New narratives can be constructed about self, others, and life, and clients can then embark on a new positive life path. People are then liberated from their past shackles, and open to use their creative free will to make their positive life choices. A key ingredient to client-therapist relationships is presence from therapists. Clients can grow from the experience of their therapist being fully present with them- a new experience many clients did not obtain from parents. For clients to experience being fully paid attention to, feeling important to their therapist, feeling their interest, and seeing in the eyes of their therapist that he/she is valued, is for many people a totally new consciousness.

Belief perseverance is the enemy of neural plasticity
Cozolino, p.164.

This means that holding onto old beliefs stops us from change, and stops us from being open to the new that exists in the here and now.

C. Rogers' books are excellent to read for more on the subject of the impact of the therapeutic relationship.

🍂🍂🍂🍂🍂

Chapter Fifteen
Our Thoughts Become Reality

As ye think, so shall ye be Bible.

*What ever you ask in prayer, believe that you have
received it, and it will be yours.*
Mark, 11:12.

From the above very brief discussion about our brains we
see they do have plasticity, are not fixed and hard wired, and they
can change. This now raises the question, How do we use our
brains, our minds? What do we want/need to do with our minds?

The quotes from the Bible above point to the fact that our
thinking process is important. Quantum physics is now confirm-
ing what was written years ago in the Bible. Our thinking does
affect our lives, and what we create. W. Dyer uses the saying, 'I'll
believe that when I see it' in reverse, 'I'll see it when I believe it',
which is more appropriate.

Quantum physics now has discovered that our thinking has
an effect on matter. What we focus our attention on changes physical reality. We can create what we want by using our attention,
our intention, our consciousness, our minds. The reality is that we
have been doing this for ever, but for many, not consciously, or not

positively.

Lynne Mc Taggert, in her new book *The Intention Experiment,* (2007), presents study after study, and extensive research that has been and is being done by renowned scientists at many of the prestigious universities from many parts of the world. These numerous studies are proving that our intentions do affect matter and create our reality, both positively and negatively. The effects of many healers have been studied scientifically and the results have proven that their intent to heal others does work. Scientific experiments have proven that our beliefs do influence materiality. I find this exciting.

We must now start to understand that our constant negative thinking has profound effects on ourselves, others, and our planet. We are all connected, we are one, we affect each other. The universe is connected by an all-encompassing quantum energy field. I'm sure you have all had the experience of walking into a room where there are negative feelings present. Maybe two people have been angry at each other: you can sense the vibe, you can feel the presence of negativity. We can't read each others' minds (at least not completely yet), but we do often feel others' feelings and sense their moods. I'm sure you all know when your partner is upset about something, or when your children are sad or angry.

We all now need to take responsibility for what we are 'putting out there'.

All emotions, beliefs, and judgements we carry in our heads and hearts are being manifested in some way. If I, for example, believe something such as, 'I am stupid, people don't like me, life is hard and lonely', then I will cause that to show up in my life. If I believe, 'I am getting old, and therefore I will not be healthy, I can't do things anymore', then that will probably become my reality. If I think judgementally about another person, then my projections can put that energy onto them, and make them behave that way, and it will also in some way harm myself.

I don't believe that every time we get sick, or when children are sick for example, that it is always that we have created it; but we don't know all the facts about how or why things happen at times. We can make a huge difference by taking responsibility for our thoughts and changing our thinking to positive directions.

Many years ago I experienced how this works. There was a time in my life that money was a problem. Never seemed to be enough. That was a belief that I brought from my childhood that I did not realize I was continuing to manifest. During this particular period, it seemed bills were coming in every day that needed to be paid. I remember thinking in despair, 'Every day a bill for $100 comes in.' Sure enough, for many days bills came in that amounted to around $100. I finally saw what was happening, and changed my thinking to, 'I have very few bills, and plenty of money to pay them.' The bills stopped coming in daily, and within some more time, as I used that affirmation, my old money script belief was changed, and I now have created an abundance of money in my life. My long held script did not change overnight, but it did change with my repeated change of thoughts.

Joe Dispenza's book *Evolve Your Brain*, (2007), is an excellent source on this topic. I'll review a few of his ideas here. He talks in detail about how he and others healed themselves of serious illnesses and conditions, by using their minds. All of us, I am sure have heard about people curing themselves of cancer, or going into remission, by the use of positive thinking; or others who have defied all odds and recovered from conditions that doctors did not believe were possible. Dr. Dispenza describes how he did just that. He poses some interesting questions for us to consider and it appears from many scientific studies that the answer to these questions, yes.

> *Is it possible that the seemingly unconscious thoughts that run through our minds daily and repeatedly, create a cascade of chemical reactions that produce not only what we feel, but also how we feel?*
> *Can we accept that the long term effects of our habitual thinking just might be the cause of how our*

body moves to a state of imbalance, or what we call
disease? Is it possible that Mument by Mument,
we train our bodies to be unhealthy by our
repeated thoughts and reactions? (Dispenza, p. 2).

Dispenza also says that our thinking, what we put our attention on, ultimately defines us and what we create. It affects us on a neurological level. 'It is where we place our attention, and on what we place our attention, that maps the very course of our state of being' (p.3).

We need to pay attention to what we are thinking, rehearsing, worrying about, expecting, fabricating, projecting and thus creating. This all becomes who we are.

We can now learn to create a new life for ourselves. We have the power to dream, to plan, to make goals and manifest those in reality, and to share that with others.

Deepak Chopra, in his book, *Quantum Healing* (1989), talks about how the cells in our bodies are constantly renewing themselves. When we believe, for example, 'I have a bad back he suggests that we program new cells to be 'bad back cells.' Thus we maintain the back problem. Our thoughts affect our bodies through neuro-peptides. They are not thoughts but they move with thoughts (p.95). Think of a scary situation, perhaps being confronted by an angry or dangerous person. Now notice your body sensation; you probably feel a rush of adrenalin. This was caused by you thinking the thought, which triggers the neuro-peptide reaction of carrying the message that releases the adrenalin. If it was a real situation, the adrenalin would be useful to defend yourself. In this same way, all of our thoughts affect our body, either positively or negatively.

Wayne Dyer, *Real Magic*, (1992), also teaches us that we have unlimited potential, that we can create our own reality by using our minds correctly. There are divine forces that work with us. We can tap into this force by quieting our minds and listening. There are many books that can help and guide you on learning to use your mind. I could easily get lost in wanting to write about them all. *The Course in Miracles* is a wonderful one. However, I will refrain from going through my entire library, and instead let your own inner guidance, or spirit, lead you to what you need to read. Your path is unique to you.

The main message of this book is that you can take charge of your life you can make a difference for yourself and our planet by changing the way you use your mind. Become aware of your thoughts, watch for the negative beliefs and judgements. They will only manifest more negativity into your life. Change your thinking to positive thoughts, beliefs, and ideas. Or better yet, learn to be silent and make room for spirit to talk to you, to guide you.

Chapter Sixteen
Ideas from
What the Bleep do we Know?

A movie that was very popular in recent years was, *What the Bleep do we Know?* I imagine most of you reading this book have seen it. If not, it is very informative about Quantum physics and how our thinking affects us and our world. I'll review some of the ideas from the movie here. Firstly, Quantum physics and mechanics are extremely hard to understand. Scientists usually say they are somewhat baffled by what they see happening, and don't understand all there is to know yet. So we nonscientists can be excused for not understanding it completely. It is very mysterious. What is discussed clearly is the power of thought and how we all, every day, are affecting ourselves, and our world, by our thinking. Why do we continue with repeat behaviours, doing the same thing, choosing the same type of partner, getting the same kind of job, having the same kinds of things happen to us over and over? Because that is what we believe and expect and therefore that is what we create.

In reality, there is a field of all possibilities, waves of possible outcomes to each occurrence that we could choose from, but we tend to choose the same one, unconsciously, because we don't know there are more possibilities, and we tend to choose what we know. As soon as we put our attention on one possibility, others disappear and the one we have chosen becomes manifested. We may think, 'Here it is again, or here I go again, same thing all over'.

What I have been experimenting with in my mind is attempting to become aware of other possibilities that could occur in any given situation. Then I decide which one I would like to choose; I do that and watch as it manifests. Very exciting at times. Try it. Think in the morning of your day ahead, and instead of thinking, 'Oh, it's Monday, work will be hard, or boring, I know what is going to happen today' think of all other possibilities that could happen. For instance, I can decide, 'I'm going to have an interesting day today'. Decide how you would like it to be different. You don't have to work out details of how it will happen, just decide what you want and let the universe create the way it will happen. I have experienced that the universe, spirit, energy, or whatever name you want to put to it, creates the events in wonderful mysterious ways for the materialization of what I choose.

The one drawback to this is I have a limited knowledge of the possibilities. I can only know what I have experienced before. Can it be possible to ask the universe to show me other possibilities that I have not experienced yet? Can I ask in the morning, 'Bring me a day that is a totally new and positive experience?' that is the focus of my new experimenting.

We must now become aware that what is happening inside us, our thoughts, emotions, beliefs, expectations, become what we see on the outside. We used to think the opposite way, that the outside world was there, fixed matter, solid, and that we had no possible influence on it. In fact the opposite is true. What appears to be solid matter is not: it is constantly moving space, atoms, and molecules, and we do have an influence on it simply by giving our attention to it, and if we add our intentions, we can create changes.

There have been many very interesting experiments and research done on what has been called the 1% effect. The studies come from the Maharishi University, and from Transcendental Meditation. When enough meditators amounting to 1% of a given population, are sent in to a troubled city someplace in the world, and all they do is check into a hotel and meditate, the effect is that violence reduces, crime lowers, accidents are less frequent, hospital admissions are lower, and the city becomes more peaceful. A recent study was done in Washington DC. The meditators met with police and told them they would lower crime rate by 25% within a few days of meditating at hotels. The Police did not believe that was possible, but in fact that is what happened.

As I mentioned earlier, Lynne McTaggert (2007) also presents a multitude of research studies that show similar results, and she is organizing thousands of people around the world, myself being one, to take part in an intention experiment (September, 2008) to lower violence. The results January 10, 2009 E-News, show that 'the experiment may have been pivotal to hasten the end of the war, which now appears imminent' L. McTaggart.

It has been known for many years that when 1% of monkeys learn to do something, that knowledge is picked up by other monkeys, even though the other monkeys have not been present to see the original group of monkeys do the new behaviour. It seems that thoughts and knowledge are passed between minds on a telepathic level. Many Aboriginal or indigenous cultures can do this very well. They can pass information between them over many miles.

Does this mean, as many are saying, that when the world has 1% of the population meditating or practising some form of positive spiritual mind control, the world will become a safer, calmer, more peaceful and loving place? We could try it and see.

The movie *What The Bleep Do We Know* presented the work of Mr. Emoto from Japan, who experimented with the effects of words or thoughts on the crystallization of water. He showed that positive words such as 'love', and 'thank you' placed on containers of water, formed molecules in the water into beautiful crystals. An important point in the movie was when one man said to the star of the movie, Marlee Matlin, 'If words can do that to water, imagine what words can do to our body'. Since our bodies are largely water it's an important question to think about. Speaking positively about ourselves and others has an affirmative effect.

An important final point is that we need to watch how we think. Often, we may think a positive affirmation, and start with a positive intent, but then erase it with a negative such as, 'This is silly, this won't work for me'. As we continue to work with positive thinking and intent and see the new positive results, then we will become more trusting of the process and learn its truth. It may take some time, so persevere.

❦ ❦ ❦ ❦

Chapter Seventeen
Review of *The Secret*

    A recent popular and interesting movie and book that many are watching and talking about is *The Secret* (R. Byrne, 2006), which presents The Law of Attraction and how we can use it to manifest what we want in our lives. I have found this interesting, although I have some reservations with it, and want to share my ideas and thinking about *The Secret* with you in the hope that it will also help you. My reservation about *The Secret* is that it focuses too much on material aspects of manifesting. Creating wealth or material possessions is not, to my mind, the most important aspect to lasting happiness.

        The secret is the law of attraction!

    Everything that's coming into your life you are
attracting into your life. And it's attracted to you
by virtue of the images you're holding in your mind.
It's what you are thinking. Whatever is going on in your
mind you are attracting to you. Every thought of yours
is a real thing - a force.
        Prentice Mulford (1834 - 1891) p.4.

What is this law of attraction? It has been with us from the beginning of time, and it determines directions in our lives and the universe. Many distinguished people have known about the power of thinking and been writing about it for centuries. It is not new. The law of attraction says like attracts like; so as you think a thought, you are attracting that to you. If you think negatively about something or someone, that is what you will attract to you and manifest. We become what we think about most, and attract what we think about most (John Assarf, p. 8). 'Thoughts become things' (Mike Dooley, p. 9). 'See yourself living in abundance, and you will attract it. It works every time, with every person, (Bob Proctor, p.12). These are all noted presenters of ideas in *The Secret*.

Most people are thinking about what they don't want rather than what they do want, and then of course they get what they don't want. We have to become aware of what we are projecting, and ensure that we create positive intentions. Looking at some principles, the law does not know the difference between positive and negative, but responds to the subject. A simple example is when a person is thinking, I don't want to be fat: fat is the subject, and that is what is manifested, staying fat or fatter. The person needs to envision, 'I am a thin person.' Then thin is the subject and will become reality. Rather than thinking, 'I want to get out of debt,' which attracts more debt, ideate 'I have an abundant life.' The law does not compute 'don't,' 'not', or 'no', it responds to the subject.

Examples from the book (p. 14-15).

I don't want to be delayed, becomes I want delays.
I don't want to spill something, becomes I want
to spill some thing.
I can't handle all this work, becomes I want
more work than I can handle.
I don't want to argue, becomes I want to argue.

As I said in the first section of this book, we unconsciously like to prove what we are thinking to be right. For example, if I judge negatively about a person saying in my head, 'She is so lazy', then I am really wanting that person to be lazy so my opinion is right. Additionally, the power of projection will actually make that person be lazy. I instead need to think, 'She accomplishes a great deal', and the magic of the law will then make that person be active and productive.

Quantum physics tells us that we have created our world, and are always continuing to do so. It does not only work when we know about it - the law has been creating what we have been projecting for centuries, consciously or unconsciously. It is now time for us to become responsible and aware of our thinking, and ensure that we think so positively and constructively.

How do we start to do this? One of the most important steps is to quiet our minds. The people in *The Secret* book, and movie, encourage people, and I agree, that meditation is important. It is an excellent way to focus and still your mind. I have been practising Transcendental Meditation for 35 years, and have found it to be invaluable in my life. Meditation helps to calm our thoughts, and has many positive physical effects on our bodies.

The Secret suggests starting with an affirmation of, 'I am the master of my thoughts.' Say it often and that will become reality. You will create the knowledge that will enable you to manifest the most magnificent version of you. The possibility of that version is already within you. Decide what you want to be, do, and have, visualize the thoughts of those things, emit the frequency, and your vision will become your life (p, 23).

What a beautiful contemplation that is, and it is within the reach of us all. Write down all you want, put it in or on a place where you will see your wishes often, read it frequently and envisage them. There is a powerful technique from Imago therapy that I use often with couples called the Vision List, and it works well by using this law of attraction principle.

Directions

1. Both of you imagine your life in 3 - 5 years time, seeing it be all you want or could wish for. Imagine that you have a magic wand (which you do in your mind) and you can create your relationship and life to be just as you want. Get a clear detailed picture and wish big. No limits!

2. Each person then make a list of at least ten items that describe your perfect relationship and life in the present tense. Write the list on your own and don't show it to your partner until you are both finished.
Write in the present tense such as, We have... We are....

3. Now sit down together, and read your lists to each other. Decide which items are similar and integrate them. Usually couples find that they want pretty much the same things. If there are some differences, does the other person accept or agree to the want of the other person? For example, if one person has on their list, we work part time, is that going to be OK with the other? If one person says, we live in the country, is that going to be OK and supported by the other?

4. Put your lists together integrating them into 10 - 20 items. You can add more if you wish.

5. Now for the magic! Each week read your list out loud together, at least once, and more is better. Take turns each time with who starts on item 1, so that you are each reading each item in turn.

6. Relax, let go of the outcome, and watch the items materialize. You will manifest what you want. If an item does not become reality, it may be because you have changed your mind about it, or the timing is not right. You can change the list and add to it as you wish.

I have this fantasy that there is a huge warehouse somewhere with storepeople patiently waiting for us to ask for the goods. There is an unlimited supply of wonderful things and events for us in the warehouse. We only have to ask. The store people are wanting to supply our wishes, but we don't ask. We don't believe we deserve the good things in life, or we think negatively, 'This will never happen for me', or 'I will be too greedy'. 'I should not ask.' When, or if, we do finally ask, the store people rejoice and are delighted to give. 'Ask, and it shall be given,' says the Bible.

The secret says that if we believe we have no control over our lives, or as I talked about in the first part of this book, that life is hard or a struggle, then that is enough for us to manifest hard or negative things. It's not that we have asked for specific things like that car accident, or getting sick, for example; but in general we have asked for something bad or hard. I have a hard time with this one in cases of children being sick, or mass tragic events, and I don't understand all the reality. However, I am willing to accept that my thoughts are extremely important, and I need to take responsibility for making sure they are positive and to do the best I can with that.

> *You have a choice right now. Do you want to believe that it's just the luck of the draw and bad things can happen to you at any time?*
> *Do you want to believe that you can be in the wrong place at the wrong time? That you have no control over circumstances?*
>
> *Or do you want to believe and know that your life experience is in your hands and that only all good can come into your life because that is the way you think? You have a choice, and whatever you choose to think will become your life experience.*
> (Byrne, *The Secret*, p. 28.)

It sounds like hard work to monitor all our thoughts, but it's not really that hard once we become aware. We need to be aware of and observe our feelings, because they tell us what we are thinking. Our thinking creates our feelings.

Think a scary thought, and watch what happens to your feelings. You will notice some kind of reaction internally. Now think of something wonderful, like the love you have for your partner or children; notice those feelings. Become aware of your feelings, and when you notice bad feelings, use that as a warning that you need to change your thinking so that you don't manifest something bad. I believe the universe gives us some time to change our thinking before it dumps bad onto us as we have asked. With practice you will learn to become the observer of your thoughts as well. Watch for your internal judgements of self and others, your criticisms, and negative beliefs. Notice your thoughts and change them where you need to.

I have noticed in my life that when I did or thought something negative for some time, the universe gave me a gentle tap on the head to wake me up to make a change. If/when I did not pay attention to the tap, then I got a harder thump. Thumps got harder and harder until I learned my lesson and changed. I now try to firstly be positive, and if I slip, then I try to listen to the taps before they become thumps.

The Secret says we can use our feelings to 'turbo-charge' what we want in life. Think about what you want in life, then add how you will feel when you get it. This will transmit a powerful frequency to the manifestation you want to create. Feel being healthy, being loved, being prosperous (p.35).

The book suggests making a list of 'Secret Shifters', That means a list of things that you know will lift your feelings if you are feeling down: a walk on the beach, beautiful music, thinking of someone you love, a fun plan, funny moments, or a good memory (p 37).

The most transforming, wonderful, and creative feeling of all is Love. 'The feeling of love is the highest frequency you can emit. If you could wrap every thought in love, if you could love everything and everyone, your life would be transformed' (*The Secret,* p. 38.). Emitting loving thoughts about another person, rather than angry judgemental thoughts, effects us personally more than it does the other person. If I am thinking angry thoughts, being critical in my head about my partner, I make myself unhappy. Then if I speak the negative thoughts and become outwardly critical, I can ruin the loving feeling between us and upset our day. This is not to say that we should not ever voice what upsets us, or ask for change, but we can do it in a loving positive way. We can speak our truth assertively, with love attached to it, instead of critical judgements. Doing so is much more likely to result in the other person being willing to change, or discuss the issue with you, without becoming defensive. As I said in the first section on communication, and it bears saying again here, when we speak to another from our Critical Parent ego state, directed at their Child ego state, we are most likely to receive a Rebellious Child, or a Critical Parent response that will result in a fight. Adult to Adult, Child to Child, or Nurturing Parent to Child, with love, is the most effective way to communicate.

The Secret suggests the following affirmation to transform your life;

> *'This is a magnificent universe. The universe is bringing all good things to me. The universe is conspiring for me in all things. The universe is supporting me in everything I do, (p. 40).*

How to do all this? Start with the above affirmation and say it often so you learn to believe it. Then come back to what is directed in the Bible, 'Ask, and you shall receive.' Many people don't set goals and dreams, don't make plans, don't think about what they want in life, but simply drift through each day, month, and year, living a lifeless week to week life. They are not asking for what they want. They may believe they don't deserve better, or that they would be bad in some way for asking. How many of us were told as children, 'It's not nice or polite to ask.' 'You are being selfish if you want.' These messages are not true, throw them out. The truth is, God or the Universe, or Spirit, or Source, whatever name you wish, gave us free will. This means that unless we use our free will to ask, then the universe will not give to us.

Therefore, think about what you want, and ask for it to be brought to you, 'put it out there' as the saying goes, and then watch the magic. As you see things you ask for start to materialize, your faith in the process will grow.

An important part of the process is to receive what comes to you, and know that you deserve it. Accept it and feel good about it, and show gratitude. When we are grateful and give thanks for what we receive, we open the way to receive more. Spend some time each day thinking or even writing about all the things in your life now that you are grateful for. Doing this sends out a positive frequency. Thinking about what you are grateful for at the beginning of each day starts your day in a positive frame of mind, and you will manifest more in your life to be grateful for. Say 'thank you' often and you will create more to be thankful for.

> *Therefore I tell you, what ever you ask in prayer,*
> *believe that you will receive it, and you will.'*
> *Mark 11:24.*

There is another verse from the Bible that I now understand if I add some words to it:

> '*For the one* (who recognizes what) *who has,*
> *more will be given, and from the one who has not*
> (believes that don't have) *even what he has*
> *will be taken away.*

I think this is saying, when we see our glass half full and are grateful for that, more will be given to us, if we see our glass half empty; and believe we have little, then we will be asking to remain in the position of lack.

Visualization is a powerful tool to use with what you are asking for. Create a clear picture or thought in your mind. Many athletes have discovered the amazing power of visualization. They have learned to 'see themselves' doing perfect dives, jumps, swims, whatever before their event, and then when in their event, that is what they do. Visualizing what you want sends out powerful frequencies and the law of attraction will bring those pictures back to you in reality. Think about the fact that every object in our lives was someone's thought or picture first. Your house, car, clothes, etc. were in some person's mind, and then they designed and created it. So we have to think of what we want first, before we can materialize it. W. Dyers' phrase, 'You will see it when you believe it',comes back to my mind. A simple but powerful technique, suggested in *The Secret* book, is to make yourself a vision board. I use a cork board that I can pin things to. Find pictures of what you want, write what you want on a postie, use pictures of people in your life that you want a loving relationship with, be creative, pin all these to your board, and they will become reality at the right time, and in the right way. Have fun with it. As you receive things on your board, give gratitude, then you can take that one off and put something else on the board. I also have an envelope that is marked, 'Thank You For'. I put the things that I have received into this and give thanks for those. It's a wonderful technique to teach children, so that they learn the law of attraction and learn to take responsibility for their life.

Pay attention to your intuition and instincts. This is something that I have learned along the way, and am still learning to follow more each day. If you have a feeling about something, no matter how small, follow it. It is the universe helping you, and bringing you what you want, need, and have asked for. A small example is when I am shopping, and have a feeling that I need to buy an item; at the time I may think, I don't need this, however invariably, I later find that I do need it. Trust the Universe, and take one step at a time. You don't need to know the entire future path of how things will come. The Universe will do that. Be willing to live in the mystery.

Expectation is a powerful attractive force.
Expect the things you want, and don't expect
the things you don't want.
> *Byrne,The Secret, p. 93.*

Life always reflects our beliefs.

What we believe about the world is how it
will always be for us.

There is one energy field, one consciousness, and we are all a part of that oneness. We are all one and connected. There is not an us and them, or an out there and in here. It is all one and the same energy. It is very important for us to realize that truth. We need to know we are all one, and stop conflicts and wars. An image I often have is of a tree with branches on all sides. Think how ridiculous it would be for branches on the east side of the tree to fight with and destroy branches on the west side. Or branches on any side to fight amongst themselves. Eventually the tree would destroy itself and die. This is what we are doing on our planet to each other, and we need to wake up and stop doing that before we do destroy ourselves.

My wish is all who read this book will ask for world peace, focus our conscious minds on creating world awakening to the fact we are one. If enough of us awaken, we can create the required change. In the field of consciousness, as quantum mechanics tells us, there is a field of all possibilities. When we use our conscious minds to ask, we will instruct the universe to materialize what we have asked for. Asking for love and peace can bring that into reality.

Enough of science, let us move on to other topics.

❦❦❦❦❦

Chapter Eighteen
Happiness, Spirituality,
Full potential, Ministry in Life

True Happiness is ... to enjoy the present,
without anxious dependence upon the future.
Seneca

True happiness involves the full use of
one's power and talents.
John W Gardner

We now arrive at the questions, Where to from here? What do you want to create in your life?

If you have discovered you've been holding on to negative baggage from your past, my hope is you have decided to drop it. Keep the positive growth you have derived from it, and drop the negative. If you are holding negative beliefs from the past, about yourself, about others, and about life, change them to positive ones. Put aside all from the past that does not serve you well. Be aware that all that has happened in your life has made you who you are. Those experiences have given you many positive abilities, strengths and opportunities, and are now part of your character.

You can now move on.

At this point I want to say I have been talking a great deal about positive and negative aspects of life, and in fact everything has both. In all things we view as positive, there are also negative aspects or outcomes, and in all things we view as negative there are also positives. For example, I can consider my early belief about life which was, 'Life is hard'. While that did create many difficult things for me to deal with (until I changed it to, 'Life is wonderful, an exciting adventure'), the positive advantage I got from that belief was that I learned to work hard. That in itself has two sides. On the positive side working hard has gained me success, and on the negative side, I at times worked too hard, and had to learn to balance my life with fun time.

Dr. J. Demartini, in his Breakthrough Experience workshops, introduces an excellent way of looking at things in a neutral light. For every negative issue that has been presented to you from life, or a difficult person in your life, ask yourself the question, how has this also been a benefit to me? For example, something that used to annoy me from other people was laziness. I changed that during the workshop with Demartini when I wrote down at least twenty reasons how laziness in others was a benefit to me. Such as, when others are not doing things all the time it gives me permission to not be working hard and doing things all the time. They show me that life does not end if things are not done, people don't have to be perfect, I won't get into trouble if I don't get things done at once, and so on. Then the next step, (and this was a hard one for me) was to identify times when I was lazy. My first reaction was of course, Not me, I'm never lazy! And of course I am at times. Becoming aware of that and seeing that I am, brought me to compassion and understanding for others.

I was invited, by Demartini, to look at how my laziness was a benefit to others. (Another hard one.) I could see that, in fact, people are often more comfortable around a relaxed person. Overly busy people often cause those around them to feel guilty for not being as busy. When I do things quickly, it deprives others the chance to perform and feel a sense of accomplishment. I would grab at things first to raise my own self-esteem, not recognizing that others might enjoy doing those things. On an even more hurtful level there is the game of Got You' where a person does everything before others have a chance, and then blames and persecutes others for being lazy and irresponsible, thus reinforcing the doer's belief of, I'm OK and you are not OK.

I invite you to try this exercise. Make a list of others' behaviours, or people that annoy you, then look at the list of 'negative' things they have done. List many reasons how each has been a benefit to you. Next, list times when you have been the same, and how your being that way has benefited others. For more details read Demartini's book or attend his workshops. In summary, what I am saying is all that has happened to you, no matter how bad, has also had some positive benefits for you. Change your thinking and move on. Don't stay stuck in old patterns of thinking such as, 'I can't do that or be that because I had a bad childhood, It's not my fault, it's their fault, If it was not for... I could be different.' You can now be and do what you choose. Forgive the past.

You now know your brain can change, that you have the power to change how you see things, and that you can create and manifest what you want in life. Consider the more positive side to life and how to get what you really want. One comment I would like to make about *The Secret* is that to my way of thinking it focuses too much on the material aspects of life. Money, houses, cars. In our western society we tend to think material things are the most important achievements, and that they will bring us happiness. 'I will be happy when I get a new house, a new car, that new job, have a million in the bank, get the right partner, have the perfect body.' Then when those things are acquired, we often find happiness is short lived, and does not last. There is nothing wrong with acquiring material possessions, do so and enjoy them, but don't think they will bring you lasting happiness. They don't. Many studies have shown that people who have won the lottery, after a few months, are back to their prior state or mood they held before their big win.

The Dalai Lama, and Buddhist philosophy, as well as many

other spiritual teachers, from Jesus onwards, say that the purpose of life is to seek happiness, and that happiness can be achieved through a process of training the mind. 'All beings naturally want to avoid suffering as much as possible, and gain happiness - that desire is innate; it doesn't have to be learned' (Dalai Lama & Cutler, p. 47). The question arises, what is happiness and what brings it to us? The subject of happiness is now a recognized field of scientific study. Dr. Martin Seligman has written a book (*Authentic Happiness,* 2002), based on positive psychology that discusses many aspects of happiness.

Probably most of us, at some time in our lives, have been caught up in the belief that material or situational gains will bring us happiness. As I said, research has shown these accomplishments or gains only bring fleeting happiness. There is nothing wrong with acquiring material possessions; just know that real happiness is not contained within those gains. Real happiness starts in the mind from a calm mind filled with gratitude for the gifts that you have.

M. Seligman (2002, p, xi) says 'authentic happiness comes from identifying and cultivating your most fundamental strengths and using them every day in work, love, play and parenting.' Constant thinking of wishing, worrying about what we don't have, brings dissatisfaction and unhappiness. Our comparing mind and judgemental thinking makes us unhappy. 'Happiness is determined more by the state of one's mind than by one's external circumstances, conditions or events' (Dali Lama). The well known homily, *looking at your life as a glass half full, rather than a half empty glass,* illustrates this well.

> *If you judge people (*or your life*) you have no*
> *time to love them (*it*)*
> *Mother Teresa*

If a person compares himself favourably with one person, he may judge he is better than him and he may then feel 'happy' (or is it really superior) temporarily, but then another unfavorable comparison with a person will make him 'unhappy'. A person can get lost in constant comparisons. 'I'm not at the top, but at least I'm not at the bottom. I'm not skinny, but at least I'm not fat. I'm not a billionaire, but at least I'm richer than them.' This thinking wastes our lives and makes us unhappy.

A wise person in my life said, 'Take it (life) as it comes.' Easier said than done, I have found, but I have found it to be true. The Dali Lama says the more reliable method to reach happiness is not to have all that we want, but rather to appreciate what we do have (1998, p. 29). As I was talking about gratitude before, being thankful for what we do have brings us a happy peaceful mind, and the universe then brings more into our lives to be thankful for.

When we think and believe, 'I have so much in my life to be grateful for,' then the law of attraction continues to bring more things to you to be grateful for. That is the life condition you are asking for. If on the other hand, we think and believe, 'I don't have what I want in my life; projecting a poverty mentality, then the law of attraction will continue that situation for us because that is what we are asking for. Our unconscious mind does not differentiate between positive and negative; it focuses on the subject and that is what becomes manifested. So if the subject is 'not enough' then a 'not enough' situation will continue. We have a mind, and can train our minds how to think, and that will achieve happiness.

E. Tolle, a popular writer on spirituality, and others talk about learning to 'be here now.' Be in the present Mument, live life fully in the now, not in past or future. Something else I heard along the way, and not sure from where: 'The past is history, the future is a mystery, and the present is a gift. That is why it is called the present.' Real happiness comes from leading a good life, living a life aimed at win/win with others. Win/win means wanting others to get what they want, as much as your getting what you want. It's not about exploiting others, taking from others or the planet in a destructive way. It is living an ethical life.

Positive emotions of love, joy, affection, glee, closeness, pleasure, serenity, contentment, hope, ecstasy and compassion bring feelings we enjoy. We need to cultivate these feelings and emotions and find what brings us happiness. That probably will be something different for each person. What I enjoy might not be what you enjoy. I do think our goal is to reach our full potential, whatever that may be; and again, that will be different for each person. Importantly, it does not mean that we will eliminate so-called negative feelings of anger, sadness, fear, boredom, etc. Those feelings are a part of life that we need to learn to live with at times; however we do need to know that when we are in those feelings they do lower our vibrational level, and we do need to learn to overcome them.

Remember, all feelings have a positive side to them. I tell my clients who come to therapy saying, 'I need to stop being angry', that anger can be helpful. We feel anger because it signals that something needs to change. Anger produces change. It is *how* we deal or *behave* with anger that may need to change. Using violent or hurtful behaviours because of feeling anger is not acceptable. When feeling angry, discuss it, ask for the change you want, then drop the anger. Don't hold onto it for hours or days. All emotions can be helpful. Sadness for example, helps us heal from grief, and scare is very important because it keeps us safe; however, irrational fears from the past are not needed.

Happiness comes from creating for yourself a meaningful life, finding your purpose, reaching your full potential, and living from your ethics and using your core strengths.

> *Your purpose is what you say it is. Your mission is*
> *the mission you give yourself*
> *Byrne, The Secret, Walsch, p. 177).*
> *When we take action in the things that truly matter*
> *deep in our hearts, when we move in directions*
> *that we consider valuable and worthy, when we*
> *clarify what we stand for in life and act accordingly,*
> *then our lives become rich and full and meaningful,*
> *and we experience a powerful sense of vitality.*
> *R. Harris, p.15.*

Finding Your Bliss

What is bliss? Bliss is often spoken about in spiritual writings as something to strive for. Feeling blissful is feeling happy, content, satisfied, feeling in 'heaven' with what we are doing. At work, or in any action, when we feel blissful, we will be enjoying ourselves, be lost in the Now of the Mument, be engrossed in what we are doing, and we will do it well, because we are enjoying ourselves. I believe each person was born with certain traits, skills, abilities, strengths and drives, guiding them towards what their purpose is. Purpose is what people are meant to be doing here in this life on this planet. Our challenge is to find what that is, and be willing to fulfill the calling from the intelligent spiritual universe. We will know we are on the right track when we feel bliss with what we are doing.

When working with clients, and they are trying to work out what they want to do with their lives, they say things like, 'I don't know who I am, or what I want' I ask them the question, 'What did you most enjoy doing when you were a child?' That is a place to start to find out where your bliss lies. The saying, 'Follow your bliss', is good advice, and you need to find your bliss. What brought you joy as a child? What did you most enjoy doing? What activities do you, or did you lose yourself in where time gets lost? What are you good at? What skills do you have? What have you always felt you wanted to do? What values are important to you? What do you stand for? Your answers to these questions will point you in the right direction.

Imagine it's your eightieth birthday, and all your friends and family are there. They are giving speeches about you and your life. What do you want people to say about you, and about the life you led? What kind of person do you want them to be saying you are? What are the qualities that make you, you? We all need to live in the Now according to our values, using our core strengths, being our unique selves, reaching our full potential so that when we are eighty, people will speak of us with love and respect.

It is not necessarily what you think you should, or must do, but what you *want* to do. The answers to those questions are a start if you are still working it out. As you start to ask, 'What brings me joy, What is my path?' The universe will answer and show you.

Reading List Suggestions

There are many writers of books on the market talking about happiness and how to get there. I would like to muse over some of their ideas, as well as mine, and I will list some good books that I have read in the bibliography.

Firstly, one of the most important aspects to happiness and feeling good about yourself is to live an ethical life. Buddhism and other major religions all teach basic principles of ethics to live by which are fundamentally the same for all. I doubt anyone would argue that these principles are wrong. For a start they lead to a peaceful mind free of guilt. I am sure that most of you reading this book live according to these basic ethics as much as possible, without self-expectations of perfection.

The basic ethic of not killing is probably the most important one, but we seem to continue to do. Wars in the name of God, in my opinion, are ludicrous. I also worry about our society that seems to enjoy seeing so much violence on TV, video games, and movies. What is that saying about us? Why do we enjoy watching violence? What are we teaching our children? Seeing so much violence, in my opinion, desensitizes people and gives the impression that violence is OK and/or to be expected (Gregory, 2005).

One hypothesis I have about why people seem to enjoy watching violence is that it feeds their addictions to drama and excitement. Remember when I talked earlier about people who were raised in families that frequently had anger, scare, sadness, and dramas, and how they became addicted to the drama and excitement. Watching violence, I feel, gives them a drama fix. Finding a more wholesome avenue to excitement would be preferable. Maintaining the negative addiction to anger and dramas may well continue manifesting that in one's life. I feel we would all be happier if we lived without violence. Peace is what each person wants.

Killing of course is on many levels. The range can be from killing a person, to killing a bug, damaging our planet, harming ourselves or others. The list could be endless, and I'm not here to tell you where to draw your own line. That is for you to decide. I certainly am not perfect on all levels. I do think we would be happier, and well served, if we become more aware of where we kill and harm, and attempt to reduce that where we can.

Other important ethical principles are being honest, not stealing, having loving kindness towards others, and being generous. Not stealing and being honest are also on many levels and can take many forms from robbing a bank to taking a pen from the office, for instance. Being honest in our relationships with others is a large part of it. However, there are of course times when it is kinder or less harmful not to tell the truth. 'What do you think of my new hairdo? may be a time to fib a bit. Most of you will have seen the slogan, 'Practice random acts of loving kindness'. We have all experienced the happy feelings when we do something kind for others. Dr. Sonja Lyubomirsky, professor of psychology at the University of California, and a noted researcher for positive psychology, designed a research study where test subjects were instructed to perform five acts of random kindness for one day a week for six weeks. The result was that their levels of happiness dramatically increased.

Generosity is an ethic, and a core strength that also takes many forms and brings a positive feeling to us, as well as others. It does not always have to do with money. Giving away material items we no longer need or use, giving of our time to help, giving love and friendship, are examples of the many ways we can be generous. Cultivating a peaceful mind brings happiness, and I have talked about this earlier in terms of how we view life. In addition, following our ethics brings peace of mind and contentment. I am sure most of you know and follow these ethics to a fairly high standard. They are part of our rules, laws and culture. I believe it's good to be reminded of them now and then.

Dr. M. Seligman (2002) has written brilliantly about happiness, and there is now an International Positive Psychology Association of which I am a member. This association is focused on furthering the science of positive psychology.

Let us look again at what Seligman says: 'Authentic happiness comes from identifying and cultivating your most fundamental strengths and using them every day in work, love, play, and parenting'. What are these fundamental strengths? He lists six core virtues as:

Wisdom and knowledge
Courage
Love and Humanity
Justice
Temperance
Spirituality and transcendence   (p,11)

These virtues can be broken down into twenty-four strengths. For example, wisdom can be broken down into strengths of curiosity, love of learning, originality, social intelligence, and the capacity to be loved as well as love. His book and web site, **www.authentichappiness.com** has a complete questionnaire for you to discover your core strengths. I urge you to find out what your core strengths are. You may of course have a good idea already. The exercise I gave you above which asked about the traits that make you, you may well reveal your core strengths. When we use our core strengths every day, the positive feelings that arise from that bring authentic happiness. It is through this action that we will reach our full potential, and obtain lasting happiness. Most of us know when we are behaving from our 'good self,' when we are putting into action those skills and traits that we are good at, and living from our core values and ethics. I'm sure we have all experienced a 'high' of emotion at those times. We feel good about ourselves and feel happy. We can consciously choose to be this self daily.

Dr. Seligman goes on to draw a distinction between

pleasures and gratifications, both of which bring happiness, but in differing ways, and differing durations. Pleasure comes from delights that have sensory and emotional components, such as thrills, excitement, orgasm, comfort, physical sensations from a hot bath, a massage, etc. They involve little thinking. Gratifications are activities we like doing, and we get absorbed in them. We feel gratified when we accomplish something and do it well: conversation, an athletic skill, reading a good book, dancing, preparing a good meal, etc. We need to frequently use our core strengths to achieve gratification. Good feelings with gratification last longer than the feelings attached to pleasures (Chapter 7).

The components of gratification are:

> The task is challenging and requires skill.
> We concentrate.
> There are clear goals.
> We get immediate feedback.
> We have deep, effortless involvement.
> There is a sense of control.
> Our sense of self vanishes.
> Time stops
> Seligman, 2002, p. 116.

Dr. Seligman discusses an alarming increase of depression that logically one would not expect to be present in wealthy countries since quality of material life is high. Interestingly, he theorizes that depression is caused in these countries because they have become nations of shortcuts to happiness and pleasure: television, sex without love, drugs, excesses with consumerism, overeating, obsessions with sports, etc. We have created so many shortcuts and labour saving devices that we don't have to use many of our skills and strengths. We are rarely presented with challenges that we can feel gratified for solving or accomplishing.

I have often thought it rather nonsensical that we now have all the labour saving mod cons that make our lives easy; and as a result, we have to go gyms to exercise since we don't use much energy to get through our days. Pushing a lawn mower or washing clothes by hand was good exercise. I remember forty years ago when I came to Australia from America, and had few of the mod cons I had left behind. I was surprised that I felt a high sense of gratification that I was capable of doing without those gadgets and machines. I had expected to feel deprived. Instead, I felt gratified when I accomplished tasks that required my skills and strengths. Too many shortcuts, says Seligman, 'sets one up for depression. The strengths and virtues may wither during a life of shortcuts rather than choosing a life made full through the pursuit of gratification' (p. 118).

The final chapters of Seligman's book discuss how we can make our lives and work much more satisfying by finding out what our core strengths are, and then finding ways to use them daily. This will create not only a happy life, but one filled with gratification as well. Even a boring routine job can be transformed into a fulfilling one by creatively thinking about how we can use our strengths.

Dr. Russ Harris (*The Happiness Trap,* 2007), discusses some interesting ideas about happiness and how it can be achieved. He begins by saying most of what we have thought about happiness in the past is not helpful, is erroneous, and that we are caught in a 'psychological trap'. Happiness elludes us, and depression is on a rapid increase as we are told. Why? As discussed above, we are caught up in wanting more and more material possessions thinking these will bring happiness. We then find through experience they do not bring lasting happiness. Happiness has two meanings. Firstly it can be pleasure, gladness, and gratification. Secondly, it is living a full and meaningful life (p.15). What Harris is saying here is similar to what Seligman, myself, and others are saying.

My experience is that feelings do not last forever, they come and go, and in fact that is necessary for us to enjoy moments of happiness. If we felt happy all the time, we would have nothing to compare the feeling to. To know what happiness is, we also need to know what unhappiness is. We need duality so we can experience opposites. We need light/dark, up/down/ happy/unhappy etc.

to know each.

Dr. Harris also says that feelings of happiness don't last; they slip away. The more we pursue and attempt to make them last, the more anxious and depressed we will feel. Once again, Dr. Harris says much the same as Dr. Seligman: 'The other meaning of happiness is "a rich, full and meaningful life." When we take action on the things that truly matter deep in our hearts, when we move in directions that we consider valuable and worthy, then our lives become rich, full and meaningful, and we experience a powerful sense of vitality,' (p. 15). During our journey in creating this full and meaningful life we will experience the full range of feelings: sadness, anger, joy and happiness. We will fail if we try to be happy all the time. All feelings and experiences bring us learning and gifts.

Dr. Harris also advocates living by our personal values, and not being driven by our thinking or feelings. This I feel, goes along with what I have said in the first part of this book. Our old beliefs and feelings are outdated, and often prevent us from being who we want to be now. We need to see them for what they are, old unhelpful stories.

Dr Harris offers techniques for dealing with these old thoughts and feelings. I recommend Dr. Harris's book, and have found it useful for myself and in working with clients. I find it validating that so many writers are now on the same wavelength, saying the same sorts of things. I think this is reflecting our universal awakening.

Chapter Nineteen
Manifesting What You Want in Life

Many writers have for years been talking about our ability to manifest what we want in life. Books by Wayne Dyer, Deepak Chopra, John Demartini, Joe Dispenza, *The Secret,* Colin Tipping, Movie of, *What the Bleep Do We Know,* Greg Braden, Eckhart Tolle, and myself, have all been promoting the idea. Not only is this true, but we in fact have been manifesting our lives for years, mostly without awareness. As I have discussed in detail in this book, our old belief systems have been creating our lives forever unconsciously. It's now time to awaken and take charge of what we create, consciously.

The first step is to ask yourself is, what do I want? I hope by now you are aware that happiness is what we all deserve, and what we are all striving for. The big question is, what makes us happy? As many have continuously preached, lasting happiness does not only come from material possessions and pleasures. By all means create an abundance of money and material possessions and enjoy them, but don't stop there. Know that what will bring you lasting happiness and gratification are creating purpose, living according to your values with integrity, meaningful work, goals, reaching your full potential. These will require you to use your strengths and skills on a daily basis. Accomplishing them will bring you gratification, and a rich full life. In short, living a good life brings happiness.

We need not only ask for what we want from the universe, but also ask what the universe wants from us? We are spiritual beings having a human experience, we are all one, we are here for a purpose. We are here to learn lessons and come back to our oneness. Our purpose is to bring consciousness to our lives by being aware and awake to the Now. We need to become autonomous, and regain our capacity for awareness, spontaneity, and intimacy, living life with integrity. To live an autonomous life involves living a life with integrity, a life of wholeness, and union with all that is. We need to re-gain our functional capacity for awareness, spontaneity and intimacy, and keep developing those (Mellor, *TAJ Journal*, 2008).

As Berne said, 'Awareness requires living in the here-and-now, and not in the elsewhere, the past or the future' (Berne, 1964, p. 158). I notice the similarity of what Berne was saying then, and what Tolle and others are saying now. We need to be grounded in the Now. Spontaneity is a joyful and wonderful quality of acting from the Now space, from our I-am-ness, rather than from our egos. We then bring the 'divine within' into life here on Earth. 'Spontaneous people are usually open, natural, and uninhibited' (Mellor, 2008, p.8). Intimacy is something many have difficulty with. Berne felt that few people had more than a few hours of true intimacy in their entire lives. Intimacy involves being open to others, being aware of what is going on inside us, and merging with others' experiences (Mellor, 2008, p. 10).

We in the developed countries live in a reasonably abundant universe that enables us to create as we choose by using the law of attraction. We have been given free will to choose how we will live. Will we learn by living right? Will we learn to love and reach happiness? Win/Win? When we learn these lessons and live positively, with integrity, then we reach/become Love. We need to learn the lessons of choice; what are the results of each choice we make? Is that what we want? Are the choices we make leading us to who we want to be? These are questions we need to consider.

Because we have been given free will, choice is in our

hands to a large degree. We will learn the consequences of our choices, both positive and negative, as we move through life. All lessons are valuable to us.

Once again, quantum physics tells us that we are all the same matter, and that this matter is reactive to our consciousness. We live in a field of all possibilities, and by using our conscious thoughts we can create and manifest. Once we have decided what we want to ask for and create, what are the steps?

Many writers and movies like *The Secret* are giving us directions to create our lives by using the law of attraction. It appears that our collective vibrations are rising to a level that we can and are manifesting at a more rapid rate. Once we clear our old subconscious negative beliefs we can move consciously to create positives in our lives.

Tipping's book, *Radical Manifestation* (2006), offers instructions on how to manifest. You can take a complete course in Radical Manifestation on his web site. **www.radicalforgiveness. com.** You will find that most of the writers on spirituality today are all saying pretty much the same. I think this is because of what Jung many years ago called our collective unconscious. We are all connected, and thinking similar ideas. I also think at this time we are experiencing a more rapid awakening, and a raising of vibration that connects our minds even more. Universe, I feel, is guiding us in what to write and do.

I will give you in detail my own process for manifesting that has worked for me for more than ten years. Tipping also acknowledges that many people have core-negative beliefs that need to be cleared in order to manifest positives in your life. He describes what I have said in the games section that when people stay locked in blaming, resentments, fear, guilt, shame, anger, and being a victim, their ability to manifest positives is blocked or restricted (2006, p. 5).

Process to Manifest

Step 1. To begin to manifest we need to be aware that there is abundant energy in the universe, and we live in a field of all possibilities.All things are possible and there is no shortage of abundance, and we all deserve abundance. Quantum physics implies that consciousness creates matter. As I have said, we need to know what we want and why we want it in order to manifest it. All of the many people talking about manifesting say that our requests need to be clear and detailed.

Step 2. You need to take another look at how old false beliefs need to be cleared so that they stop blocking your progress. Still not sure what your old beliefs might be? Look at what is present in your life, what keeps turning up over and over? What patterns are being repeated? Your beliefs may be creating these patterns. Visualize having abundance now in your life, envisage that you have now received all that you dream about, and happiness is all around you. Look at the details of that, what changes it has made in your life. Now feel deep inside yourself, how do you feel having obtained that abundance? Search for any resistant feelings and beliefs. Ask yourself some questions here.

What belief might it prove for me when I *don't*
have what I want?

What fears might I have about *having* what I want?

What will I feel about myself when I receive what
I am asking for?

Complete this sentence.

I am committed to my present situation of lack, or not having_____ _____because it gives me_____ or proves_____ _____or protects me from_____.

You could write in your journal about this. Give yourself plenty of time to explore all resistant feelings and beliefs. They have most likely been blocking you.

Let me go through something in more detail, that I experienced many years ago. When I visualized manifesting an abundance of money in my life. I would feel some fear. The belief system I used to hold was, I have to do all the work, life is a struggle. So not having money proved life was a struggle for me. Therefore I was unconsciously committed to not having money because it maintained my victim position, proved life was hard work as my Mom and Dad said, and protected me from an idea that my life would be boring if not working. I also found a fear of what others would think of me, and what changes it would make in my life. It took a while to change these beliefs and I have done so now.

There are a variety of beliefs that might be lingering in unconscious recesses of people's minds. 'I don't deserve to have abundance or be loved, Life is not meant to be easy. I try hard, but things just don't work for me. If I have lots, others will miss out, I will be selfish'. If you find any of these or similar, I invite you to redecide now. They are not true. You could waste your life holding onto these beliefs. Speak to the universe out loud, and voice your willingness to let go of any old negative beliefs. It is important at many steps along the way to speak your intentions out loud. Something about doing that gives it more energy, and raises vibrations.

Step 3. Have an honest look at any destructive behaviours you may be using such as over drinking, drug use, destructive relationships, sabotaging success by not working, creating accidents, creating dramas to feed your addiction to anger, sadness or fear. Making bad choices in life blocks success. Are you willing to begin to change or modify these behaviours? Living with integrity is vital.

Step 4. Forgiveness. Be willing to forgive yourself and others for any past wrongdoings. Tipping has a good program for Radical Forgiveness on his web page. I recommend that to you. Know that all people and events in your life were brought to you for learning and growth. At some level all things have been a benefit to you, even if negative. Experiences have made you who you are today with many gifts. You have developed skills, strengths, and understanding from those experiences.

Keep in mind that whatever a person has done to you, you may have also done in some way to others - perhaps to a lesser degree but, none the less, have enacted it. We are all capable of violence and abuse. We all have a dark side inside of us when we honestly examine ourselves. We have all executed hurtful things to others at times.

Forgive, drop the past. You need a clear energy field to manifest. It does you no service to hold onto past grudges.

Step 5. Decide what you want to manifest. This takes time and careful thinking. It is important to be clear and careful about what you ask for.

There is a mythical story of King Midas who wished to have everything he touched turn to gold. He got his wish, but then could not eat, since everything that touched his lips turned to gold. Consider the below areas in your life and what you want in each area.

Step 6. Make your lists.

There are many ways you can make your lists of what you will manifest. I find it helpful to work in several categories. We want all areas of our life to be working well, and be in balance. For example, having an abundance of money does not help much if the rest of our lives are in disarray. Consider what you want in these areas.

Material possessions.

Physical.

Intellectual pursuits.

Personal growth.

Spiritual growth.

Financial.

Family.

Friends.

Relationship.

Work.

Hobbies and leisure time.

Global wants for all people and
our planet.

What I want to give to the universe.

Think about each area (you may think of other areas) and decide what you will manifest. Notice I say, 'what you will manifest' and not what you want. It is now important to work in the positive present. If we say to the universe, I want_____. We will in fact be asking to stay in the wanting stage rather than receiving. 'I want to lose weight,' means the person will always be 'wanting to lose' rather than, 'I have lost weight'. Make your lists using positive language. I Now have_____.
I have manifested_____.

Does your list fit with your values and morals? Think of your integrity; do they match? Will what you manifest require you to use your signature strengths and skills? Remembering that using these will bring you gratification and happiness. For myself, I would not be happy having nothing to do all day, every day. I like to be creative and active, and growing in intellectual and spiritual pursuits. Think about what you like to do with your days.

You can if you wish put some time frames to your lists. I

use a 3 - 1 - 5 time line. What I will have in my life in three months, in one year, and in five years' time. Be clear about the details of what you list.

People will have different types of desires on their list, and I believe Maslow's hierarchy of needs is a way of understanding this. Maslow, a noted psychologist, constructed a framework to understand human needs. At the base of the hierarchy are bodily needs of food, shelter, sleep, warmth, and sex. These needs are primary, and are required to be met before a person is comfortable moving on to higher needs. At the next level are security needs of protection and safety. Then come needs of belonging, being part of a family, community, friendship, and relationship. After those needs are met a person may focus on esteem needs of respect, approval, dignity, moving up to self-actualization, and then transcendence.

Therefore, if a person does not have their basic needs met, they will want to manifest at that level. Home, food, security will be their focus. Others who have those needs met will then be focused on the higher needs of relationships, love and self-esteem. When those are met, a person may be striving for self-actualization, spiritual growth and connection to spirit. This level comes sometimes not until later in life, as Jung talked about. It usually takes the first half of life to meet the first three to four levels of needs before one can aspire to higher levels. All needs are fine, and it is important to manifest at levels that are right for you.

Step 6. Visualize having each item on your list. It is best to work with only one or two at a time. See or think about it in detail. Some people visualize by seeing pictures or images, and some people do it by thoughts. Either way is fine. Don't worry if you are a person who does not see pictures. Many don't, myself included. A clear idea is fine. Allow yourself to experience your feelings that go with having what you are manifesting. Enjoy the new picture of you and your life. Allow yourself to think of the benefits for you and others, of having your dreams materialize. This will help neutralize any left over resistances. If there are sounds attached to your picture, imagine hearing those sounds, imagine colours, and include any aroma that might belong to your picture. It is helpful to include all five senses.

Visualizing has been proven to be very effective. As mentioned, sports people have been using the technique for years. When they visualize the perfect performance before their event, the subconscious mind does not know the difference between image and reality, therefore when the sports person then executes their event they are more likely to perform as per their visualization.

One final aspect to visualization, is to share it with your partner perhaps, but as a rule don't broadcast to many others. Doing that evokes the ego, and ego gets in the way. An attitude of, 'Look how great and powerful I am, I can manifest', does not serve you well with the universe. An attitude of being humble and grateful serves you better.

Step 7. Put voice to your list. This is a proven technique from Imago relationship therapy. The Vision list, which I discussed earlier, is used with couples to create their vision of a perfect relationship. They are instructed to read their list our loud several times a week. This results in visions becoming reality. Using this same principle, read your list out loud a few times. Check to see if you have any lingering resistances, and if so, say out loud that you are willing to heal from those. You may also want to use a peg board of some description as I described earlier. Put your items on your board in some creative way. Pictures or words, whatever feels right for you.

Step 8. Hand it over to the universe in faith. Trust in spirit or universe to bring you what you have asked for, or even better, with perfection for you, and in perfect timing. Don't hang onto your requests. Now is the step to let go of attachment to what you are asking for. I know this is hard. Think about how it is when you order something from a catalogue. You order it, and then let it go, trusting that it will be delivered. You don't keep re-ordering items on a daily basis. Continuing to re-order daily holds you in the ordering phase, rather than the receiving position.

Trusting universe with how and where is essential, without judging, or insisting on your agenda. You need to hand it to universe and then go on with your daily life. The universe is constantly moving us towards growth and healing, so trust that all is going according to plan. We don't know the big picture, universe does, and therefore knows better what is best for us. Trust in that knowledge.

> *Those who are certain of the outcome can afford to wait,*
> *and without anxiety Course in Miracles.*

My example of this was about ten years ago when we had a property in the country. I loved the location, but wanted a better house, and wanted some water close by. I visualized a house to be on that location. There was a creek, but a larger amount of water just was not in the area. I was deciding to forget about water since I loved the location. I thought no more about it. Over years our situation changed, and we had to sell the property. If I had received my house on that location I would have had to leave it. We then lived in another house. Again situations changed and we sold. We now live a beautiful house, with a verandah looking out at the country (as I visualized), a creek in front, and a near a river where I have a boat. It took me some time to recall my earlier visualization, and realize that I had gotten better than what I had initially visualized, a perfect location, beautiful house, water, and at the perfect time. In addition, amazing events occurred during the entire process to ensure the property came to us.

Step 9. Plan your actions.

When I say, 'hand it to the universe', that does not mean sitting back passively, doing nothing, and thinking the universe is going to do it all for you. It's not going to be brought to your door step while you wait. I have learned, sometimes the hard way, that universe will only meet our requests if we do our part. I think we have to put in 100% effort, and then spirit or universe will meet and help us with its 100% of energy. When you have made your list, read it out loud, and handed it over to universe, then make plans of action of what you will do to help manifest what you are ordering.

Over my many years, for example, I have wanted different career studies, and achievements. I had to do my part by taking action by enrolling in courses, doing the work, studying, writeing the thesis, etc. Along the way universe cleared paths for me. Courses became available at the right time, I was accepted into graduate schools, I was given good teachers and markers, doors opened. I was guided in many ways. Extraordinary events happened to help me.

When you take your steps of action, and the doors open for you, then you will know you are on the right path. If doors do not open then you may need to change direction until doors do open. Listen to the still voice or feelings inside to guide you.

> *When one door of happiness closes, another opens,*
> *but often we look so long at the closed door that*
> *we do not see that one has been opened for us.*
> *Helen Keller*

Step 10. Gratitude.

Constantly being grateful for gifts universal spirit gives us is essential. We need to have an attitude of thanks for our gifts, rather than one of just taking. When we see our life as being abundant we will continue to manifest that prosperity situation. When divine spirit hears our gratitude, it appreciates our thanks, and feels inclined to continue giving. By being grateful, we are demonstrating our knowledge of being one with God, with universe, with divine spirit. Nothing is to be taken for granted, and gratitude expresses our love to spirit. 'The nature of gratitude helps dispel the idea that we do not have enough, that we will never have enough, and that we ourselves are not enough. When your attention is on scarcity, you are telling universal spirit you need more, and are not grateful for all that you have' (Dyer, 1997, p. 149). Practise each morning and evening spending a few minutes being grateful for all the gifts and blessings in your life.

Chapter Twenty
Reaching Your Full Potential &
Finding your purpose

This final chapter is the culmination of all I have been saying. I feel the below are the most important points I want to make. Our growth in this area is vital to ourselves as a whole, and to our planet, which are one and the same. We will now return to an aspect of Transactional Analysis that I discussed before, which is our capacity for being and doing, and our capacity for awareness. Where do they meet, and where do they differ? All three are fundamental to our spiritual growth.

Earlier suggested questions are, What does the universe want from me? What is my path, my purpose? Why am I here? Many of us, I'm sure, have asked those questions, and more. I believe we need to consider what service we can provide for ourselves and others. What service will be of benefit to others and the planet, and bring us gratification, and happiness? As we learn to extend our gratifications we will naturally move toward wanting to give of ourselves in some way. We live here with others, and giving and receiving are a vital aspect of our being. We need to both give and receive. To receive we need to give, and to give we need to receive. Many people have difficulty with one or the other. Some are very good at giving and helping others, but not good at asking for help, or receiving from others. Other people are takers and want to receive, but not give generously. Being of service in some way is important, and it does not have to be on a large scale. Helping a friend, raising children, doing our job, being a loving partner, whatever is fine. It's 'how' we do it that matters. Do we do it with full attention, presence, awareness and love?

When you learn to manifest fully, you will find that you will naturally move towards wanting to be of service, and will leave your ego behind. 'Your well-being, which is the purpose of your manifesting practice, is genuinely and inextricably connected to the lives and well-being of others' (Dyer, 1997, p. 164). A paradox of manifesting is that the more we are of service to others, the more we grow in unconditional love, the more is manifested in our life.

Being and Doing

Learning to 'be' in life, in full awareness, is our main purpose. Arising out of being, our doing will be guided.

> *Can human beings lose the density of their conditioned mind structures and become like crystals or precious stones, so to speak, transparent to the light of consciousness? Tolle, p. 5.*

Our life has a purpose of both being (Tolle calls inner) and doing (Tolle calls outer). Being is our primary purpose, doing is second-ary. Our being purpose is to awaken, to become aware. To live in the state of being, being aware and awake, bringing consciousness to the world, listening to our inner voice, our inner feelings, being aware of what is going on inside. From that state we will be guided to our outer or doing purpose.

That lesson has been a difficult one for me, and I suspect for many of you. I have always been such a doing kind of person. Always doing something, not often sitting still, always thinking ahead, 'What do I need to be doing next?' I developed this mode as a survival tactic when I was young. I believed I had to be one step ahead to stay out of trouble, and be safe. Sound familiar to anyone else? I did acquire many gifts from that experience. I learned to be very organized, developed a high energy level, and clear thinking; but I lost touch with knowing how to just be.

From reading Tolle's books (which I highly recommend), I have learned to be, and listen inside to what my next direction is for work, and my life. I now see that I have been 'guided' in each step of my life and work, although I did not recognize all of it at the time. Many times in my life I have experienced 'becoming aware, or hearing' an idea to do something, My energy would then be high, and I felt 'driven' to complete whatever it was. I enjoyed what I was doing, and doors opened. I now still at times need to remind myself that I am safe, and I can 'be' and listen, rather than getting lost in my thinking.

Thinking is usually about past regrets, shame, blaming, or judging, or worrying about the future, and it is the ego striving to survive and maintain its hold on us. Awakening takes us away from our constant mad monkey thinking. As Tolle says, awakening happens to us, and we cannot make it happen. To attempt to force is an action of the ego. We strive for enlightenment to be our most prized possession.

I do however think we can practise being, watching, listening and living in the Now as much as possible. Daily meditation is very helpful to experience times of pure consciousness, to become aware of the space between thoughts. Being aware of the space between thoughts is blissful. It is there, in that space, that we find the 'I -am' of who we are. I am not my thoughts, I am the being that can watch my thoughts, and watch the space between my thoughts. That is the 'being' state.

What's so important about 'being' you may ask? Many people think, 'If I just "be", I will become lazy and get nothing done.' I used to ask the same question, and surmise the same about 'just being'. Just 'being' to me felt like doing nothing. The state of being is not always inaction. We can be busy doing what we need to, or want to be doing, and at the same time, be in a total state of being with our actions. That means, whatever you are doing, be totally present, and aware of your actions. You have no doubt experienced times when you were so totally engrossed in what you were doing that you lost yourself in that. No other thoughts intruded into your mind; time stood still. You were totally present and enjoying what you were doing. Practising being present in the Now, I feel, will bring us towards awakening. So at times practise sitting in the state of 'being' either awake, or in meditation. Also when you are performing some action, practise being with your actions totally. Once you have had a taste of it then you will know it, and can make a conscious choice to be fully present, rather than lost in your thoughts.

> *Opening yourself to the emerging consciousness and*
> *bringing its light into this world then becomes the*
> *primary purpose of your life*
> *Tolle, p. 261.*

Being fully present, in the state of being, allows the energy of pure consciousness, the energy of intelligent universe, spirit, God, whatever name you wish to use, come forth into your life, and this world, more totally. We become a channel for pure consciousness to enter this world. That is our most important purpose for being here. We then become connected to the universal energy; but more descriptive is that the universal energy has access to us, and through us to this world. From that state of being, we will become aware of what we need to be doing. Keep in mind that at times what we need to be doing, is to 'Be' and allow space for consciousness to flow through us. Pure consciousness affects all matter. Through our projecting positive intentions from our state of Being we can change and heal our world. We simply radiate the energy of love.

Our society has a definition of success that pushes us towards material gains. There is nothing wrong with material gains, but there is more than just that. Don't get lost in the crazy world of recognition, money, and material as being the most important. Enjoy them, but there is more to life. Success is in the present moment, living life to the full. Full living is in taking the step you are taking in the Now, give it your fullest attention 'what the future holds for you depends on your state of consciousness now' (Tolle,

p. 217). Your purpose will come through awareness, not through thinking (Tolle, p. 273).

Be awake to what happens in your life. Chance meetings of people, someone giving you a message, a door opening, something a person says to you, a book falls off the shelf towards you, an intuitive feeling from inside you, all may be guiding you towards your next step. Listen for the still small voice inside. There may well be times you feel uncomfortable with this stillness, not knowing where you will go next or what you will do next. Your ego will certainly not like it. Given time you will learn to live with uncertainty, in fact turn it into wonder, and relish it.

> *If uncertainty is unacceptable to you, it tuns into fear.*
> *If it is perfectly acceptable, it turns into increased*
> *aliveness, alertness, and creativity*
> Tolle, p.274.

In summary, our purpose, reaching our full potential, is to be aware, awake, and present to each moment. The Now of life is allowing pure consciousness to channel through us into our world. Consciousness will guide us, inspire us, lead us to our required service and action, and bring love to our world, within us, between us, and to all matter. We need to stay aware while in action as well as in stillness.

What will it mean to bring consciousness to our world? Being fully present and aware, looking at, being grateful for, and appreciating each other, nature, pets, plants, flowers, trees, birds, rivers, our entire planet, brings nourishment from our conscious awareness. Living a good life, giving and receiving love, I believe will fill our lives with blessings and happiness. What changes can we bring to our planet when we do that?

This day and your life are God's gift to you -
so give thanks and be joyful always.
                    Jim Beggs

Bibliography

Berne, E., *Games People Play*, 1964, Penguin Book, Ltd. Middlesex, England.

Berne, E., *What Do You Say After You Say Hello*, 1972, Corgi Books, London UK.

Bader, E., & P. Pearson, 1988, *In Quest of the Mythical Mate*, Brunner Mazel, Inc. New York, New York.

Bowlby, J., *Attachment,* 1971, Pelican Books, UK.

Byrne, R., *The Secret*, 2006, Atria Books, New York.

Course in Miracles.

Chopra, D., 1989, *Quantum Healing*, Bantum Books, New York.

Clarkson, P., *Transactional Analysis Psychotherapy,* 1992, Tavistock/Routledge, London.

Cozolino, L., 2002, *The Neuroscience of Psychotherapy,* W.W. Norton & Company, New York.

Gary Craig, www.emotionalfreedomtechnique.com

Dali Lama and H. Cutler, 1998, *The Art of Happiness*, Hodder, Sydney.

Demartini, J., *The Breakthrough Experience*, 2002, Hay House CA, USA.

Dispenza, J., 2007, *Evolve Your Brain, Health* Communications, Florida, USA.D.

Dyer,W., 1992, *Real Magic*, Harper Collins, NSW, Australia.

Dyer, W., *Manifest Your Destiny*, 1997, Harper-Collins, USA.

Erskine, R., *Theories and Methods of an Integrative Transactional Analysis*, 1997, TA Press, California.

Erskine, R. and M. Zalcman, Jan 1979, *Transactional Analysis Journal,* ITAA California, USA.

Fryba, M.,*The Art of Happiness, Teachings of Buddhist Psychology,* 1987, Shambhala Publications, UK.

Gregory, L., *Preventing Domestic Violence by Promoting Non Violence*, 2005, Fremantle Publishing, W.A. Australia.

Gouldings, R. & M., *Changing Lives Through Redecision,* 1997, Grove Press, New York.

Harris, R., *The Happiness Trap,* 2007, Exisle Publishing Ltd.

Hendrix, H., 1992, *Keeping the Love You Find,* Pocket Books, New York.

Imago Relationship Therapy, http://www.imagorelationships.com/

James M. and D., Jongward, *Born to Win,* 1983, Addison-Wesley Publishing Co, Philippines.

M. James, M.*The Inner Core*, 1981, Transactional Analysis Journal, p. 54 - 65, ITAA.

Krishnamurti,J., (1965),*Krishnamurti's Talks, Krishnamurti Writings,* Inc, Ojai, California.

McTaggert, L., *The Intention Experiment*, 2007, Free Press, New York.

Mellor, K., *Autonomy with Integrity,* Transactional Analysis Journal, 2008, Vol. 38 # 3.

www.biamenetwork.net

Michie, D., *Buddhism for Busy People*, 2004, Allen & Unwin, Australia

Joy, a Book of Quotations, 2000, India.

Redfield, J., *The Celestine Prophecy*,1993, Bantam Books, Australia.

Redfield, J., *The Celestine Vision*, 1997, Bantam Books, Australia.

Schore, A. *Affect Regulation*, 2003, W.W. Norton & Co. New York.

The Secret, 2006, Movie, Prime Time Productions, Australia.

Seligman, M. *Authentic Happiness,* 2002, Free Press, New York.

Steiner, C., *Scripts People Live*, 1974, Bantam Books, Grove Press, New York.

Stewart, I., & Joines,V., *TA Today*, 1987, Lifespace Publishing, North Carolina, USA.

Tipping, C., *Radical Forgiveness*, 1997, Global 13 Publications, GA, USA.

Tipping, C., *Radical Manifestation*, 2006, Global Publications, Inc, Marietta GA, USA.

Tolle, E., *A New Earth*, 2005,Penguin Books, Victoria, Australia.

Movie, The Secret, www.The Secret.

Mararishi Mehesh Yogi, *The Science of Being and Art of Living,* 1966, MIU Press.

ABOUT THE AUTHOR

Linda Gregory has been a clinical Transactional Analyst and trainer for over 25 years in Perth, Western Australia. She came to Australia in the 60s from America.

Linda has been a Board member of both the International and Regional TA Associations, and has been a presenter at Conferences worldwide.

Linda's Ph.D. thesis in sociology focused on domestic violence, and explored changes to scripting as preventative measures. Linda has become increasingly drawn to the aspect of Spirituality and integrating that with TA.

Linda lives and practises now in a sea change town just South of Perth with her husband. She has three adult children and their partners, and five grandchildren.

Also published; *Preventing Domestic Violence by Promoting Non-Violence*, 2004.

You can contact Linda through
www.drlindagregory.com.au

E Mail... lgregory@iinet.net.au